EVERYDAY

Peace

Spiritual Refreshment for Women

PATRICIA MITCHELL

BARBOUR
PUBLISHING

© 2012 Barbour Publishing, Inc.

Writing and compilation by Patricia Mitchell in association with Snapdragon Group℠ Editorial Services.

Print ISBN 978-1-62836-636-5

eBook Editions:
Adobe Digital Edition (.epub) 978-1-63058-051-3
Kindle and MobiPocket Edition (.prc) 978-1-63058-052-0

Published by Barbour Publishing, Inc., P.O. Box 719, Uhrichsville, Ohio 44683, www.barbourbooks.com

Our mission is to publish and distribute inspirational products offering exceptional value and biblical encouragement to the masses.

ecpa Member of the
Evangelical Christian
Publishers Association

Printed in the United States of America.

Contents

Introduction 6

Accountability 8

Adversity 10

Affliction 12

Age 14

Anger 16

Anxiety 18

Appearance 20

Authority 22

Bereavement 24

Bitterness........... 26

Blame 28

Broken Heart........ 30

Change 32

Children............ 34

Competition......... 36

Conflict............. 38

Contentment 40

Courage 42

Coworkers 44

Criticism 46

Daily Walk 48

Danger 50

Deceit 52

Delay............... 54

Depression.......... 56

Disappointment 58

Discipleship......... 60

Discouragement 62

Divorce............. 64

Doubt 66

Emotions 68

Emptiness 70

Enemies............ 72

Estrangement 74

Eternal Life 76

Failure 78

Faithfulness........ 80

Family............. 82

Fear................ 84

Forgiveness 86

Friends............. 88

Future.............. 90

Giving.............. 92

Goals............... 94

God 96

God's Will.......... 98

Gratitude 100

Guilt 102

Honesty 104

Hope.............. 106

Humility........... 108

Illness 110
Indecision 112
Intolerance 114
Jealousy 116
Leadership 118
Life's Purpose 120
Loneliness 122
Loss 124
Marriage 126
Materialism 128
Miscarriage 130
Misjudgment 132
Mistakes 134
Money Matters 136
Morality 138
Motivation 140
Obedience 142
The Past 144
Perfectionism 146
Perseverance 148
Prayer 150
Pregnancy 152
Pride 154
Principles 156
Priorities 158
Provocation 160

Rebellion 162
Regret 164
Relationships 166
Reputation 168
Responsibilities 170
Risk 172
Sacrifice 174
Scriptures 176
Self-awareness 178
Service 180
Singleness 182
Speech 184
Spiritual Struggle . . . 186
Starting Over 188
Suffering 190
Surrender 192
Temptation 194
Tiredness 196
Traditions 198
Trials 200
Trust 202
Violence 204
Work 206

Let me hear what God the Lord will speak,
for he will speak peace to his people, to his faithful
to those who turn to him in their hearts. . . .
Steadfast love and faithfulness will meet;
righteousness and peace will kiss each other.

PSALM 85:8, 10 NRSV

Introduction

*"I leave you peace; my peace I give you.
I do not give it to you as the world does.
So don't let your hearts be troubled or afraid."*

JOHN 14:27 NCV

Wherever we look, there's chaos instead of calm, uncertainty instead of assurance, war instead of peace. Even within ourselves, we find struggles of heart and spirit as we try to make sense of our emotions and experiences, our fears and losses. Yet despite the turmoil without and within us, peace is possible.

God sent His Son, Jesus, into the world to bring you genuine and lasting peace. Through His power to renew and restore, He eases your anxieties with the balm of forgiveness. He opens the way to a loving and sustaining relationship with your heavenly Father. With His Spirit alive in your heart, He gently leads you to His stillness.

Everyday Peace has been designed to support you as you reach out to God for serenity of heart, mind, and spirit. In each reflection, His reassuring message embraces you with comfort and encouragement. Leaning on Him, you discover that serenity is available, achievable, and yours.

Let these words and those that follow remind you that chaos does not have the final say. Let God hold you in the peace He promises to all who believe in Him and trust in His love.

ACCOUNTABILITY

Honest Admission

*If we confess our sins, he who is
faithful and just will forgive us our sins and
cleanse us from all unrighteousness.*

1 JOHN 1:9 NRSV

Few of us like to fess up to our mistakes!
We wish we could simply run away and hide
from the words we never should have said
or the blunder we never should have made.
Yet our hearts tell us that peace with others
and with ourselves comes only through
our honest admission of what we've done.
By holding ourselves accountable for our
actions, we need never run and hide but
gently move forward—humbled, perhaps,
but wiser.

Everything He Has Given

*Each of us will give a
personal account to God.*

ROMANS 14:12 NLT

God holds us accountable for the many gifts He has given us, including our time and talents, our resources and relationships. Our heavenly Father, however, is not a heartless overseer with a checklist in hand, but a loving God who desires our ultimate happiness. He knows our joy, peace, and satisfaction increase when we explore our gifts to the fullest. For our benefit, God asks for accountability, inviting us to use wisely and well everything He has given.

ADVERSITY

Ask Him

When I am surrounded by troubles,
you keep me safe.

PSALM 138:7 GNT

No matter how hard we work to avoid it, adversity rears its ugly head. It might be the result of a mistake we've made, but sometimes it's not our fault at all. Either way, the key to meeting adversity is not to dread it or fear it, but to believe in our God-given strength and abilities. Even in the middle of hardship, there is peace in knowing we can ask God for everything we need to overcome it.

Perspective

*[Jesus said,] "Come to Me,
all you who labor and are heavy laden,
and I will give you rest."*

MATTHEW 11:28 NKJV

Stay calm!" For most of us, that's easier said than done when our situation turns bad. Yet "stay calm" is wise advice. By not reacting with panic, we give ourselves the perspective we need to assess our problem and sort through our options. That's why God assures us that He is with us and ready to help us at all times. With our trust placed in His strength and power, we're able to stay calm, even in adversity.

AFFLICTION

The Great Physician

"This is what the LORD says. . . . 'I will heal my people and will let them enjoy abundant peace and security.'"

JEREMIAH 33:2, 6

Physical afflictions such as accidental injuries, recurring health problems, and serious disease may affect us as we journey through life. Though we beg God for healing, He sometimes permits our ailments to continue, compelling us to lean even more heavily on Him. As we do, His Spirit increases our spiritual understanding and strengthens our inner fortitude. Our Great Physician works in us true healing—a relationship with our loving and compassionate God—that brings lasting peace.

A Healing Balm

*Many are the afflictions of
the righteous: but the LORD
delivereth him out of them all.*

PSALM 34:19 KJV

Many maladies are not physical, but
spiritual. We might be afflicted with a timid
nature, a nagging conscience, or a heavy
heart. Perhaps we find ourselves prone to
self-defeating behavior or to overdepen-
dence on others. While these afflictions
may not be visible to other people, God
sees, and He cares. The Great Physician of
the spirit invites us to come to Him with
whatever troubles us and receive the balm
of His restorative touch.

AGE

The Age You Are

"I will be your God throughout your lifetime—until your hair is white with age."

ISAIAH 46:4 NLT

Growing up, most kids are eager to add another candle to their birthday cakes. Then all too soon, they'd rather not count candles at all anymore! Living at peace with the age we are begins with believing God has placed us in the world at the right time and in the right place to accomplish everything He has planned for us to do. Young, old, or in between, age is what we make of it!

Through God's Eyes

I was young and now I am old, yet I have never seen the righteous forsaken.

PSALM 37:25

Age discrimination touches us when our value is assessed by how old we are or appear to be. In God's eyes, however, everyone is valuable. Not one of us has more worth than another because she's in the prime of life or has hair streaked with gray. When we look at others through God's eyes, we see infants, children, adults, and seniors He adores. And when we look in the mirror, we behold the face of God's beloved daughter.

ANGER

Good Gifts

Christ died for our sins,
just as the Scriptures said.

1 CORINTHIANS 15:3 NLT

Do you know what makes God angry? It's definitely not you, no matter what you may have done or ever will do! God gets angry over sin because sin harms us and destroys the good gifts He has in mind for us. Jesus, God's Son, has accepted God's rightful wrath, and because He did, we never need to worry about seeing our God with a frown on His face. Now isn't that something to feel good about?

God-Given Passion

*Do not let the sun go down while
you are still angry, and do not
give the devil a foothold.*

EPHESIANS 4:26–27

Anger, like fire, can either harm or help. Anger harms us when it smolders in our hearts and overwhelms us with bitterness. It harms others when it flares in verbal or physical violence. But anger helps us when it motivates us to warn others of danger, speak in defense of the innocent, and take a stand against injustice. Anger is a God-given passion intended to bring us closer to Him as we strive to work His goodness in the world.

ANXIETY

Strong Arms

Cast all your anxiety on him,
because he cares for you.

1 PETER 5:7 NRSV

A physician once said to her patient, "It's not what you're eating; it's what's eating you."

Unrelenting anxiety takes a toll on our physical and mental well-being, and that's why God invites us to give our worries to Him. He has strong arms, and He can hold anything we need to put in them. One by one, we must take each thing that burdens us and give it to God. Then we can relax, knowing He has our best interests at heart.

The Prayer Remedy

I want you to be free from anxieties.

1 CORINTHIANS 7:32 NRSV

God has a remedy for anxiety, and that remedy is prayer. When we speak to Him about an issue that concerns us, we are speaking to someone who has the power to do something about it. Whether the issue is big or small, a major problem or a minor annoyance, God's ear is only a prayer away. The Great Physician longs to ease our anxiety, embrace us in His comfort, and wrap our hearts and minds in His peace.

APPEARANCE

Delightful Beauty

God does not judge by
outward appearances.

GALATIANS 2:6 GNT

Many of us spend a lot of time in front of
the mirror. We're quick to find fault with
the smallest real or perceived blemish,
and then our self-esteem takes a dive!

Yet what's really important isn't outward
appearance at all, but the appearance of our
spirit: our character, our integrity, our compassion for others. While physical beauty
fades, spiritual beauty lasts forever, and it's
the kind of beauty God delights to see.

No Mistakes!

*Charm is deceptive and beauty
disappears, but a woman who
honors the Lord should be praised.*

PROVERBS 31:30 GNT

God created each of us to be a unique expression of womanhood. He didn't intend for us to be exactly like anyone else, and no, He never makes mistakes! That our heavenly Father loves us just as we are compels us to look at ourselves through His eyes and see the beautiful daughter He sees. Why? Because when we're at peace with our appearance, we radiate the kind of confidence that is the essence of true personal beauty.

AUTHORITY

The Right Direction

*How joyful are those who fear the LORD and
delight in obeying his commands.*

PSALM 112:1 NLT

God's commandments are like curbs.
Curbs are built to keep drivers on the
road, and prevent them from swerving and
endangering pedestrians. Similarly, when
God tells us not to do something, He is
doing so for our safety and for the safety of
others. He says no to those things that would
take us away from Him and the journey He
has planned for us. It's His way of giving us
the peace of knowing we're headed in the
right direction.

Guiding Others

There is no authority except from God.

ROMANS 13:1 NKJV

Many of us are uncomfortable with authority. We may shy away from imposing rules on children in the home or fail to articulate our wishes to subordinates in the workplace. When God places us in positions of authority, however, He is entrusting us with the privilege of guiding others in the same way He guides us, and that is with compassion, kindness, and understanding. Authority is ours not to build up ourselves, but to build up others in love.

BEREAVEMENT

Comfort

Though I walk through the valley of
the shadow of death, I will fear no evil;
for You are with me; Your rod and
Your staff, they comfort me.

PSALM 23:4, NKJV

When we lose someone we love, the pain cuts deep. Sometimes it last for years; and even after decades have passed, the wound still aches. Right where it hurts is where God desires to soothe and comfort us. He yearns to assure us of His continuing presence in our lives, and to strengthen us with confidence in His unfailing wisdom in all things. Even in the depths of loss, our peace rests with Him.

Just the Beginning

You have changed my sadness into a joyful dance;
you have taken away my sorrow and
surrounded me with joy.

PSALM 30:11 GNT

God allowed Himself to experience the pain of bereavement when His Son, Jesus, suffered and died for us. In Jesus' resurrection, however, God showed us that death is not the end, but the beginning of our new lives with Him in heaven. Yes, God understands our most profound grief, and He wants us to find peace in believing this great truth: The power of death lasts only awhile. Life in Him continues forever.

BITTERNESS

An Invitation

*Don't let anyone become bitter and
cause trouble for the rest of you.*

HEBREWS 12:15 CEV

Drop a speck of dirt into a glass of clean
water, and the water is no longer fit to
drink. Dirt and purity cannot coexist, and
neither can bitterness and peace of mind.
That's why God invites us to come to Him
with whatever makes us feel the least bit
bitter, whether it's memories from long
ago or circumstances in our lives right now.
He longs to replace bitterness with blessings, resentment with rest, and anger with
peace.

A Cooling Pool of Forgiveness

Get rid of all bitterness, passion, and anger. No more shouting or insults, no more hateful feelings of any sort.

EPHESIANS 4:31 GNT

Few stories inspire more than those about women and men who have refused to let injustice rob them of their dignity. Rather than bathe in hate and bitterness, they refreshed themselves in the cooling pool of forgiveness. They have discovered how to live at peace even in the face of unfairness and undeserved animosity. It's God's way, and it's what we discover when we let His Spirit replace our bitterness with His forgiveness, our hurt with His understanding.

BLAME

Making Things Right

*[Jesus said,] "Do not judge, and you
will not be judged; do not condemn,
and you will not be condemned."*

LUKE 6:37 NRSV

When things go wrong, we want to find
out why. In our search, however, we're often
distracted by pointing a finger at other
people, and it's then that we lose the chance
to learn from our mistakes. If we let Him,
God will gently shift our search inward, and
lead us to a deeper understanding of our
motives and desires, attitude and actions.
From there we can step forward in peace to
make things right again.

God's Embrace

Before the world was created,
God had Christ choose us to live
with him and to be his holy and
innocent and loving people.

EPHESIANS 1:4 CEV

What did I do wrong?" From those plain-
tive words flows a stream of self-blame for
the rebelliousness of a child, faithlessness
of a spouse, or betrayal of a friend. It's
called a guilt trip, and it's a journey God
doesn't want us to take. Instead, He asks us
to go no further than His embrace, where
He will listen as we pour out our hearts to
Him. Let Him show the way to genuine acceptance and spiritual peace.

BROKEN HEART

Never the Same

*The LORD is close to the brokenhearted;
he rescues those whose spirits are crushed.*

PSALM 34:18 NLT

Life will never be the same again, of that
we are sure. While God doesn't promise
to shield our hearts from all pain, He does
promise to fill our hearts with His comfort.
He is a God eager to heal and to put back
together what has been broken by sin or
sorrow. No, we may never understand why
it happened on this side of heaven, but we
can accept it. We may never be the same,
but we can live at peace.

Back to His Side

*The Lord God is waiting to show how
kind he is and to have pity on you.
The Lord always does right;
he blesses those who trust him.*

ISAIAH 30:18 CEV

A broken heart is a mark of love, for only those we love have the power to grieve us. Because God loves us beyond measure, He knows what a broken heart feels like, for we have often strayed away from Him. Yes, we have the power to grieve Him, but He has the power and the will to bring us back to His side. God is ready to mend the rift between Himself and the sorrowful soul.

CHANGE

A Smooth Way Ahead

Since we are living by the Spirit,
let us follow the Spirit's leading
in every part of our lives.

GALATIANS 5:25 NLT

Change leads to anything but tranquility! Any significant life change, even a welcome one, produces stress until a new level of comfort and familiarity sets in. When we face change, we must allow God to smooth the way ahead and show us His will. After all, there's no place we're going that He hasn't been. Whether the path ahead looks exciting or scary, we can step forward with confidence, knowing our God is walking right beside us.

What Bliss!

*Jesus Christ the same yesterday,
and to day, and for ever.*

HEBREWS 13:8 KJV

In a world of constant change, what
comfort to know that God never changes!
From the beginning of time, His love
for the world has endured, and nothing
we could do will ever alter His love. His
promises remain as valid as they were
when He first spoke them, and His desire
to bring us closer to Him still burns within
His unchangeable heart. From the turmoil
of change to the peace of God's presence—
what bliss!

CHILDREN

The Next Generation

Train children in the right way,
and when old, they will not stray.

PROVERBS 22:6 NRSV

Whether or not we have children of our own, we are setting an example for the young. If there are children in our homes, they learn from us how to get along in the world—not so much from what we tell them, but from what they see us do. In public places, young people take their cue from the attitude and behavior of the adults around them. Spiritually, each of us is a "mother" to the next generation.

From Heart to Heart

*Jesus said, "Let the little children
come to Me, and do not forbid them;
for of such is the kingdom of heaven."*

MATTHEW 19:14 NKJV

The message of God's love and compassion has been passed down from generation to generation throughout history. Now it lies in our hands. The more we learn about God, the more it becomes our responsibility to share what we know with the young. The spiritual experiences that have strengthened us are the same ones that will inspire those who walk after us on their journey to holiness. God's message goes from person to person, from heart to heart.

COMPETITION

Excellence

I run with purpose in every step.
I am not just shadowboxing.

1 CORINTHIANS 9:26 NLT

If we believe competition is all about the thrill of victory and the agony of defeat, it's no wonder we might decide not to compete with others! But when we compete with ourselves to excel at what we do, to advance on our spiritual journey, and to walk closer with God every day, then we have the right idea about competition. Seen God's way, competition motivates us to become more and more the peace-loving women He intends us to be.

Prize of Eternal Life

It is by God's grace that you have been saved through faith. It is not the result of your own efforts, but God's gift.

EPHESIANS 2:8–9 GNT

Intense competition is integral to athletic events. Crowds gather to watch one team beat the other, and the winners receive prizes and all the glory heaped on those who triumph. Even winning at the highest levels imaginable, however, cannot compare to Jesus' victory over death. He won, and His win is our win. No more striving to earn our way to heaven, because He has handed us the prize of eternal life!

CONFLICT

Conflict Resolution

A truly wise person uses few words;
a person with understanding
is even-tempered.

PROVERBS 17:27 NLT

In conflicts, emotions take over. Though
we might face our foes with steely resolve,
inside we're a knot of nerves; or we're so
upset that we simply run from the fight!
God has a better way. Godly conflict reso-
lution begins with one person letting go of
emotions and approaching the other with
reason, understanding, and a will to com-
promise. It ends in peace, with a deeper
relationship based on genuine caring and
mutual respect.

A Closer Walk

Perhaps the most intense conflict we will ever experience won't be with someone else, but with ourselves. In our continuing desire to walk closer to God, we battle emotions, thoughts, and temptations that throw us into turmoil. But we do not confront these enemies of faith alone because God's Spirit fights alongside us and for us. No matter how intense the struggle, we must hold to the peace of knowing our God will prevail.

CONTENTMENT

God's Scales

Godliness with contentment is great gain.

1 TIMOTHY 6:6 KJV

When it comes to evaluating our lives, God's scales weigh differently than ours. The smallest of things can bring us the deepest joy. When we embrace our lives just as they are, we can lay down the struggle for what might be or might have been. We can discover the blessing of contentment, knowing that, for this moment, our lives are the perfect starting place for the next step in the journey.

Enough!

*I have learned to be content
with whatever I have.*

PHILIPPIANS 4:11 NRSV

Having what we want, or wanting what
we have. It's amazing the difference in
simply reordering the words! What a gift
it is to feel that sense of *enough*, to not
always be thinking *more*, to believe that
God has given what we truly need. As we
focus today on the pockets of our lives that
we "wouldn't have any other way," let's
whisper a prayer of thanks. Take a breath
and let this moment be full, just on its own.

COURAGE

When We Need It

Lord, you are my shield, my wonderful
God who gives me courage.

PSALM 3:3 NCV

We never know where courage will pop
up in our lives, because we never know
what we'll face that will require it. We
can be sure, though, that God will give us
courage when we need it. God is both our
protector and our strength. So we can be
confident that whatever we face, we do not
face it alone. We face today with resources
both from our own souls and the Spirit that
dwells within us.

Victory Is Waiting

[Jesus said,] "Take heart, because
I have overcome the world."

JOHN 16:33 NLT

While living in this world that we can
touch and see, we remember that we are
also part of a world that we know only
through faith. In the physical world around
us, there's disappointment and struggle,
for sure. But as citizens of the kingdom
of heaven, we know a greater power that
advocates for us. Jesus never claimed we
would be without struggle, but He always
reminded His followers of the victory that
is waiting.

COWORKERS

Spiritual Sweetness

*Don't mistreat someone who has
mistreated you. But try to earn the
respect of others, and do your best
to live at peace with everyone.*

ROMANS 12:17–18 CEV

When we're working among others either
at our job or elsewhere, we bring our emotions with us. Inevitably, we hear a hurtful
remark or feel slighted by someone else,
and our relationship with the group suffers. And so do we. God changes our bitter feelings to spiritual sweetness when
we respond with composure, overlooking
offenses and granting friendliness, kindness, and respect. Even if peace doesn't
reign among others, it can reign in us.

Called to Action

*Be ready at all times to answer
anyone who asks you to explain
the hope you have in you.*

1 PETER 3:15 GNT

Most of us find it easier to contemplate
God's commandments than to practice
them. Yet we're called to action, and what
better place to start than with and among
the people we work with every day? They're
the ones who will notice our willingness to
go the extra mile, our peacefulness in tense
situations, our self-control under fire, and
our respect for everyone. Our coworkers are
the ones who may ask how they, too, could
walk with God.

CRITICISM

Important Issues

*Whoever heeds life-giving correction
will be at home among the wise.
Those who disregard discipline despise
themselves, but the one who heeds
correction gains understanding.*

PROVERBS 15:31–32

When someone criticizes us, it's only natural for us to feel hurt and upset. But what did we actually hear—a mean-spirited opinion or an uncomfortable fact? To find out usually requires soul searching, prayer, and perhaps consultation with a trustworthy friend or family member. Once we understand the spirit behind the criticism, peace is ours. We can dismiss the remark, or thank the person who cares about us enough to bring an important issue to our attention.

God's Truth

We will speak the truth in love.

EPHESIANS 4:15 NLT

Should we speak up or butt out? Yes, God
would have us warn others to keep them
from harm, and yes, He would have us resist the temptation to meddle in others'
affairs. We can discern His will by knowing
our motivation. Is it to bring God's truth
to a straying person, or to bolster our own
ego at the expense of someone else? After
we've answered that question, we know exactly what God would have us do.

DAILY WALK
Deeper and Deeper

*Just as you received Christ Jesus as Lord, continue
to live your lives in him,
rooted and built up in him, strengthened
in the faith as you were taught.*

COLOSSIANS 2:6–7

We walk our spiritual walk, day after day, sometimes unsure of our progress. Nevertheless, the roots are going down. We can't see beneath the soil where God tends to our faith, but the longer we continue in the direction of faith, the deeper His hold on us. We came to Him with nothing to use as a bargaining chip, just acceptance of His love. And that is all it takes to keep walking and growing deeper and deeper.

His Daughter

What does the LORD require of you?
To act justly and to love mercy and
to walk humbly with your God.

MICAH 6:8

Day by day, the woman of God calmly and
joyfully goes about her work. She never
frets about making it to the top, for God
asks only that she do her best. She's not
distraught if she doesn't win, for God asks
only for her faithfulness. She pays no attention to what others think of her or her
place in the world, for God has called her
His daughter and blesses every day of her
life with His love.

DANGER

Detour

*I beg you to avoid the evil
things your bodies want to do
that fight against your soul.*

1 PETER 2:11 NCV

Like a flashing red light on the roadway,
danger signals from God warn us of peril
ahead. His signals may come as a troubled
conscience, a nagging suspicion that our
conduct needs correction, or a particular
verse from the Bible that speaks to us at
gut-deep level. We avoid calamity by heed-
ing His signal immediately! He will restore
our peace of mind and heart as we stop,
pray, and listen, and then follow His detour
around the hazard.

Together for Good

*We know that all things work together
for good for those who love God,
who are called according to his purpose.*

ROMANS 8:28 NRSV

There is danger ahead, say the analysts
and commentators. They warn of heated
conflicts between nations and economic
turmoil at home. Though we recognize
serious threats, we do not panic. We remember how God has helped us through so
many dangers in the past, and we rely on
His strength and protection in the future,
whatever that future may bring. We believe
He can bring good out of any calamity, because we have seen Him do it.

DECEIT

Peace of Mind

"Do not lie. Do not deceive one another."

LEVITICUS 19:11

Most of us know what it's like to be deceived by someone. Not only are we angry at the deceiver, but we're angry at ourselves for believing the person in the first place! Forgiveness for the deceiver, however, opens the way to forgiveness for ourselves. Then we can possess the peace of mind and heart necessary to face forward, using our experience to warn others and shield ourselves against any future deceptive designs.

God's Mirror

Put on your new nature, created to be like God—
truly righteous and holy.

EPHESIANS 4:24 NLT

Worse than being deceived by a friend or loved one is to deceive ourselves by thinking we can possess God's gifts of genuine and long-lasting peace, joy, and comfort while acting like God, the author of these gifts, doesn't matter. These blessings belong to us only when we have seen ourselves in God's mirror and measured ourselves by His standards—and then humbly allowed Him to clothe us in the purity and holiness offered by Jesus Christ.

DELAY

Creator of Time

Wait for the promise of the Father.

ACTS 1:4 KJV

Most of us do not like delay! We fidget in waiting rooms and grocery lines, and when we send a friend a text, we're annoyed if she doesn't respond immediately. Yes, that's us. But God is the creator of time, He knows time from its beginning to its end, and He knows where in time to grant the blessing we so earnestly desire. We pray, and wait with faith, trusting Him to say, "The time is now."

God-Given Delay

Be patient and wait for the Lord to act.

PSALM 37:7 GNT

Most all of us can name a special thing we'd like to do "someday." And the reason we aren't doing it today is because we have other, higher priorities that need our attention. Our willingness to accept delay shows that we accept God's timing for our lives and know the value of postponing those things better suited to a future year, as He wills. In faith, we can embrace God-given delay with ease and confidence.

DEPRESSION

Lean on Him

*Do not be worried and upset,
Jesus told them. Believe in
God and believe also in me.*

JOHN 14:1 GNT

It's possible to hide the symptoms of depression behind a brave face or a casual "I'm good" in reply to those who ask. But God, who searches the heart, can see the shadows of sadness that sap our strength and wear away at our happiness. He looks at us with mercy and compassion rather than judgment. He opens His arms to us and invites us to lean on Him as He soothes, heals, and comforts our hurting hearts.

The Heavenly Father Cares

I am the Lord your God;
I strengthen you and tell you,
Do not be afraid; I will help you.

ISAIAH 41:13 GNT

Depression can hit anyone, and it can hit hard. Whether we can trace it to a specific incident or not, depression's darkness can envelop us for days, weeks, or even longer. It's nothing to be ashamed of, and it's nothing to ignore. We all have people in our lives who can and will help, if given the chance. If we don't have family or friends nearby, we can take advantage of resources in our communities. And no matter where we are, there is our heavenly Father, who knows, understands, and cares.

DISAPPOINTMENT

Surprised and Amazed

*"Anyone who trusts in me
will not be disappointed."*

ISAIAH 49:23 NCV

As we spend more time thinking about God, we become aware of His work in our lives. Certain changes, openings, and opportunities that come our way leave us feeling surprised and amazed. When we open our eyes to all the blessings He has showered on us, our hearts fill with wonder and gratitude. As we walk closer and closer with Him, there's one feeling we'll never have to worry about—disappointment!

Every Step

*"God blesses those who mourn,
for they will be comforted."*

MATTHEW 5:4 NLT

When we don't reach the goals we set
for ourselves, we often feel disappointment. Though God may use it to turn us
toward Him and His will for our lives, He
warns against letting disappointment turn
us away from a worthy, God-given dream.
Instead, He desires to help us, strengthen
us, and encourage us. Like a personal life
coach, God wants us to succeed, and He will
remain with us every step of the way.

DISCIPLESHIP

His Disciple

*Jesus said, "If you hold to my teaching, you are
really my disciples. Then you will know the truth,
and the truth will set you free."*

JOHN 8:31–32

We may not call ourselves disciples,
but we are. The question God poses is
this: What are we disciples of? To answer
honestly, many women would have to say
romance or security, money or beauty.
Each person has to decide for herself. God
invites us to become His disciple. Our
"yes" means we put Him first in all things.
It means we walk in peace and contentment
with our trust in Him. This is the kind of
discipleship God has called us to.

Walking with God

I am persuaded that neither death nor life. . .nor height nor depth, nor any other created thing, shall be able to separate us from the love of God.

Our walk with God puts us in discipleship with Him. The blessing of discipleship, however, won't keep us from experiencing the bumps along the road, like ridicule or scorn, hardship or even persecution that comes as a result of our faith. And those things, too, are a blessing, because in them we know our discipleship is showing! Discipleship means we know we will never be without His presence and love, no matter how many twists and turns we encounter on the road ahead.

DISCOURAGEMENT

The Road Uphill

"Be strong and courageous! Do not be afraid or discouraged. For the Lord your God is with you wherever you go."

JOSHUA 1:9 NLT

Sometimes it feels like we're climbing uphill all the way, making little or no progress. We are encouraged when we realize we aren't alone, that many women are feeling exactly the way we're feeling. When we reach out to friends and loved ones, we can do so knowing they will understand. And we can return the favor when others look to us, when they need someone to care. The road uphill is easier when we walk hand in hand with others, and with God.

God's Mighty Power

The LORD. . .will always be
with you and help you, so don't
ever be afraid of your enemies.

DEUTERONOMY 31:8 CEV

Sometimes we're discouraged because we're focused on what stands against us. The obstacles are huge, and we consider ourselves realistic to call them exactly what they are. But if we stop there, we're ignoring God's mighty power. It's real, and it's effective. No, we cannot overcome these hurdles by ourselves, and kudos to those women who are willing to admit it. So let's call on Him to help and strengthen us. He would love to hear us ask.

DIVORCE

Today, Tomorrow, Forever

Teach me the way I should go,
for to you I lift up my soul.

PSALM 143:8 NRSV

Divorce not only dissolves physical relationships but threatens spiritual relationships, too. Our relationship with God is more important than ever when earthly ones disintegrate, for whatever reason. It's true, God does not like divorce because of the heart-deep wounds it causes His people; but He loves each of us nonetheless. Now is the time to seek His wholeness and peace by asking for His mercy and trusting in His love, because His relationship with us is for today, tomorrow, and forever.

Refreshing Waters

You must get rid of all these things: anger,
passion, and hateful feelings.
COLOSSIANS 3:8 GNT

While going through a divorce is painful,
allowing resentment to linger in our lives
is worse. Resentment can last for years,
decades, and beyond within the heart that
harbors it, poisoning present and future
relationships, and undermining self-
confidence and inner peace. Genuine,
heart-deep forgiveness is the only remedy for the bitterness, hurt, anger, and
animosity divorce so commonly leaves in
its wake. With forgiveness, the refreshing
waters of renewal flow into a cleansed and
blameless heart.

DOUBT

A Deeper Understanding

You must have faith and not doubt.
Anyone who doubts is like an ocean
wave tossed around in a storm.

JAMES 1:6 CEV

Bible readers who examine what God says about His eternal love and infinite compassion often stop and ask, "Really?" It's a legitimate question and one God would like to answer. Healthy doubt compels us to ponder His claims and promises. It draws us to pray for God's Spirit to deepen our understanding and sharpen our spiritual vision. Eager inquiry, along with an attentive and receptive mind, guides us from "Really?" to "Wow!"

Promises Fulfilled

What if some did not believe?
Will their unbelief make the faithfulness
of God without effect? Certainly not!

ROMANS 3:3–4 NKJV

One of the great advantages of studying
the Bible is discovering how God, from the
beginning of time, has followed through on
His promises. Though some of His promises have yet to be fulfilled, why would we
doubt them? God does not change, and He
has never proved false or unfaithful. We
can accept those things in our lives that
we don't understand right now, because
there's no doubt in God's mind about His
love for us.

EMOTIONS

Extraordinary Love

I weep with sorrow;
encourage me by your word.

PSALM 119:28 NLT

Emotions can whip a woman from laughter to tears and back again in the space of an hour! While violent mood swings may indicate a need for compassionate medical attention, we can embrace our emotions by remembering they are part of the body and spirit our God has created for our good. Used rightly, emotions enable us to feel empathy, express care and concern, and reach out to others with the warmth and humanity of God's extraordinary love.

His Continued Presence

I am with you always,
even unto the end of the world.

MATTHEW 28:20 KJV

As women, we know our moods change!
That's why God, who never changes, warns
us against relying on our emotions to discern matters of faith. Instead, He invites
us to let His unchanging care, compassion,
and love for us assure us of His continued
presence, even when emotions tug at us
from all directions. His heart hears us, His
hands steady us, and His strength supports
us on the heights and in the depths of human emotion.

EMPTINESS

His Sweet Presence

Your God, the Lord himself, will be with you.
He will not fail you or abandon you.

DEUTERONOMY 31:6 GNT

We may be happily walking with God, and then suddenly we feel like we're all alone on the path. Where has He gone? Does He no longer care? It's this kind of faith-testing emptiness that works to strengthen our resolve as we continue to seek and to pray, to listen for His voice and grow in His wisdom. At the right time, His sweet presence will flood our spirits with the awesome joy of knowing He has been with us all along!

He's in Control

*Just as we have a share in Christ's
many sufferings, so also through
Christ we share in God's great help.*

2 CORINTHIANS 1:5 GNT

When someone we love is no longer in our lives, we're left with a painful hole in the center of our hearts. How we wish things had worked out differently! God desires to fill our emptiness with His comfort, understanding, and love. Despite what happened, God remains in control, and His care for us will never waver. Yes, we hurt right now. That's why He's waiting with open arms to embrace us and comfort our sorrowful souls.

ENEMIES

In Harmony

*"Do not be afraid of their words
or dismayed by their looks."*

EZEKIEL 2:6 NKJV

No matter how hard we try to live in
harmony with others, there may be
individuals or groups determined to
do us harm. While we remain watchful,
defending ourselves if attacked by our
enemies, God would have us do something
else, and that is pray for them. We pray
for His Spirit of love to soften their hearts
and enlighten their minds, because in
Him alone is true and lasting peace among
people and among nations.

Protected

*Your enemy the devil prowls
around like a roaring lion looking
for someone to devour. Resist him,
standing firm in the faith.*

1 Peter 5:8–9

Your strongest and most subtle enemies are not those you can see but those invisible to the eye. Enemies like temptation, discouragement, ungodly desires, and selfishness work to lure you away from God's path and your trust in Him. Yet through your faith in Jesus Christ, you walk protected with the shield of God's strength and power, and you rest secure in knowing God has overcome all the enemies of love and peace, purity and joy.

ESTRANGEMENT

Bridges between Hearts

*The righteous cry out, and the
LORD hears them; he delivers
them from all their troubles.*

PSALM 34:17

Estrangement happens in families and
between friends. Where once there had
been affection, now there is distance;
and though reconciliation seems far off,
we continue to love, pray, and hope. We
reach out to God, and He graciously fills
the empty spot in our hearts. Surrendering
all to Him, we find peace in the quiet
and courageous work of remaining open
and understanding, compassionate and
forgiving, for from these things God builds
bridges from one heart to another.

Welcome Back!

*Draw near to God, and he
will draw near to you.*

JAMES 4:8 NRSV

When God feels the pain of estrangement, it's not because He has strayed from us, but because we have strayed from Him. But no matter why we left or where we've gone, there's one thing we know for sure: We're welcome back. Always. God stands waiting with open arms to receive any wandering soul. He is willing to forgive, eager to celebrate our homecoming, and ready to pour out on us the renewal and refreshment of His lasting peace.

ETERNAL LIFE

Life!

*"Those who believe in
the Son have eternal life."*

JOHN 3:36 NCV

If we have never visited a place but want to know what it's like, we ask someone who's been there. Jesus, who came from heaven, is the only one who can tell us what heaven is like; and Jesus, who rose from the grave and ascended to heaven, is the only one who can take us there. With our hope and our hearts resting in His hands, we have nothing to fear, not even death. Why? Because, in Him, death means life—eternal life.

Nothing to Earn

*God's gift is eternal life given
by Jesus Christ our Lord.*

ROMANS 6:23 CEV

If God required you to earn eternal life,
you'd have every reason to worry! After all,
how would you know when, or if, you've
done enough? That's why God brings eternal life to you through Jesus. Jesus' sin-
free life means you have nothing to earn,
but only to receive, as He offers to you the
perfection He already has won. He has provided a way for you to have eternal life, and
the way is nothing other than Himself.

FAILURE

Embraced in Love

*The LORD is good, a refuge
in times of trouble. He cares
for those who trust in him.*

NAHUM 1:7

Sometimes our friendships and marriages
fail us. Sometimes we even fail ourselves
when we don't live up to our standards or
reach our goals. Yet even in failure, God
soothes us with His presence and embraces
us in His love. He's not there to judge
or point a finger, but only to support us
through a rough part of the road and lead us
in the direction He would have us go. Real
failure would be to refuse His help.

Ultimate Trust

*Because of the Lord's great love
we are not consumed, for his
compassions never fail.*

LAMENTATIONS 3:22

Despite the anguish failure leaves behind, there's something positive to take away. Amid the frequent failure of families to prosper, of health to improve, of money to bring security, and of relationships to last, God once again reminds us that our ultimate trust belongs in Him. Nothing else but His presence has a guarantee attached to it, and no earthly person or thing can promise us spiritual peace without fail. But God can, and He does.

FAITHFULNESS

God-Given Vision

Never let go of loyalty and faithfulness.

PROVERBS 3:3 GNT

Dedicated inventors and innovators are those who remain faithful to their idea, despite years, or even a lifetime, of scorn. In a similar way, our faithfulness to God's commandments and His will often attracts ridicule, because not everyone looks at life with spiritual eyes and sees what we see. Our God-given vision of forgiveness and compassion, dignity and justice, under-standing and love for everyone keeps us working faithfully to make His idea for the world a reality.

Good Choices

*The Lord is faithful, and he will strengthen you
and keep you safe from the Evil One.*

2 THESSALONIANS 3:3 GNT

When the choice before us is going along
with others or remaining true to what we
believe is right, we know which choice to
make. But knowing isn't enough! God's
Spirit working within us gives us the
strength and conviction it takes to remain
faithful to ourselves and our loved ones, to
our promises, our ideals, and our responsibilities. When acting on our good choices
takes courage, we can rest at ease in His
faithfulness to us.

FAMILY

From God

A wise woman strengthens her family.

PROVERBS 14:1 NCV

It's likely that the place we exert the most influence is right in our own family. Our day-to-day decisions, conduct, and attitude affect the lives of those closest to us in ways that may span generations. When the source of our strength and wisdom comes from God, we are like the woman who showers life-giving water on tender flowers. As they grow, beauty and sweetness surround us, and goodness and kindness flow back to us.

God at the Center

*Let the mighty strength of
the Lord make you strong.*

EPHESIANS 6:10 CEV

Where family ties are strongest, God
dwells at the center of the household.
He yearns to be the one we turn to when
pressures and problems arise, and when
arguments threaten to alienate spouses,
parents, and children. If forgiveness seems
difficult, God can smooth the way. If old
wounds still fester, God can provide healing and comfort. Strong families aren't
built by human effort alone but by God's
power and presence in our homes.

FEAR

The Abundant Life

"Fear not, for I am with you; be not dismayed, for I am your God. I will strengthen you, yes, I will help you."

ISAIAH 41:10 NKJV

Fear, as unsettling as it is, can signal danger and deter us from taking ill-advised risks. But it can also drain our energy, turn us inward, and hinder us from enjoying the abundant life God has in mind for us. He can show us how to separate healthy and justified fear from unnecessary dread that burdens our hearts and spirits. Lay destructive fears on His shoulders, and let Him surround you with His strength, courage, and confidence.

In Confidence and Peace

"Do not fear or be dismayed;
tomorrow go out against them,
and the Lord will be with you."

2 CHRONICLES 20:17 NRSV

Sometimes fear is all that's standing between us and what we long to do. We get butterflies in our stomachs when we encounter new people, interview for a job, or ask for a raise in pay. When fear blocks our way ahead, we can let God take His place in front of us, beside us, and behind us. As He opens the way, we can move forward in confidence and peace.

FORGIVENESS

The Command to Forgive

*Put up with each other, and forgive
anyone who does you wrong,
just as Christ has forgiven you.*

COLOSSIANS 3:13 CEV

In the Bible, God doesn't simply suggest we forgive others; He commands it! Why? Because without it, there's no room for authentic peace. When we forgive the offenses others commit against us, we're acknowledging that we, too, have sinned and stand in need of forgiveness. It's through genuinely forgiving others and humbly accepting forgiveness from others and from God that we come to experience true peace of mind and heart.

Scattered Darkness

I forgive you all that you have done,
says the Lord God.

EZEKIEL 16:63 NRSV

Deep within many of our hearts lies a sin we're ashamed of. We're so ashamed that we don't want anyone else to know about it, least of all God! Yet when we realize God already sees the inmost part of our hearts and yearns to shine His light of love, compassion, and forgiveness there, we're compelled to confess what has burdened us for so long. Only God can scatter the darkness and set our troubled hearts at rest.

FRIENDS

Eternal Friendship

[Jesus said,] "I have called you friends."

JOHN 15:15 NKJV

A friend is someone we can confide in, who's there for us, who cares and understands. All that and more is the kind of friend God wants to be to us. More than even our closest longtime friends, God knows where we came from, the children we used to be, and the women we are now— and He loves us through and through. His is a friendship available to us today and one that will carry us into eternity.

Bringing Hearts Together

*One who forgives an
affront fosters friendship.*

PROVERBS 17:9 NRSV

Many things can come between friends: anger, jealousy, hurt, or blame. When friends stubbornly refuse to extend their hands in forgiveness, the rift can go on for years, if not a lifetime. If there's a place in our hearts only a certain friend could fill, perhaps in her heart there's an empty spot where we used to be. God knows both, and He knows how to bring hearts together in forgiveness, kindness, and peace.

FUTURE

A Better Way

"I know the plans I have for you,"
declares the LORD, "plans to prosper
you and not to harm you, plans to
give you hope and a future."

JEREMIAH 29:11

The future is loaded with uncertainty. Some of us react by feeling powerless to make any change in our circumstances, and others by growing bitter when the years fail to unfold according to our plans. God has a better way. He invites us to know that He is in control and to put our future into His hands. He encourages us to pray and work today, and accept with gratitude all He has in store for us tomorrow.

A Better Tomorrow

What you ought to say is,
"If the Lord wants us to,
we will live and do this or that."

JAMES 4:15 NLT

When we were young, most of us lunged into the future with energy and optimism. Then, as years passed, we found that some of our plans worked out, and some did not. Focusing on today's good helps us plan better for tomorrow. And although we now step ahead with perhaps a little less vitality and a more balanced perspective, we have found that the future leads nowhere unless God is guiding and we are following His way.

GIVING

Delights

*You must each decide in your heart how much
to give. And don't give reluctantly
or in response to pressure. "For God
loves a person who gives cheerfully."*

2 CORINTHIANS 9:7 NLT

When we count our blessings, do we ever
ask ourselves why God gave them to us in
the first place? Sure, He blesses us with
everything we need for our well-being, and
also with what He delights to give us for
our comfort and enjoyment. He blesses us,
too, so we can delight in sharing our time,
abilities, talents, and financial resources
with others. In God's world, "blessing" and
"sharing" and "happiness" travel together.

True Riches

The generous will prosper;
those who refresh others will
themselves be refreshed.

PROVERBS 11:25 NLT

True riches come not from gathering as much as possible, but from giving as much as possible. Think of the warm feeling we get when we are able to help someone in need, or when we give of our time and effort to make a positive difference for others. This is the only wealth guaranteed to grow in value and the only riches certain to last a lifetime—and beyond. The more we give, the more we receive.

GOALS

Celebration

Our only goal is to please God.

2 Corinthians 5:9 NCV

When we're working toward a goal, we look forward to celebrating as soon as we reach it. But our time between now and then is something to celebrate, too. The process of planning and creating, of learning and building, is often more thrilling than achieving what we had set out to do. Yes, let's keep our eyes on the goal, but keep our hearts and minds on the miracle of every moment that we spend getting there.

Proceed in Peace

*May He grant you according to your heart's
desire, and fulfill all your purpose.*

PSALM 20:4 NKJV

Sometimes when we set an objective for
ourselves, we experience a time of inse-
curity. Can we really pull it off? At those
times, it's good to talk to God about it. Better than we do, He knows our strengths and
abilities and what we're capable of achieving. After all, He gave us the physical, in-
tellectual, creative, and spiritual resources
we possess. If we lay out our goals before
Him, asking Him for His blessing and His
help, we will feel much more confident
throughout the process. Then we can proceed in peace.

GOD

Belonging to Him

*The fear of the LORD is
the beginning of knowledge.*

PROVERBS 1:7 NKJV

Does the thought of God, with power and
authority over all things, make us tremble?
If so, it means we sense the reality of His
existence and the extent of His might—
after all, it's that might that protects us
and brings us the help we need in troubled
times. He is also the God who offers
us unconditional love, overwhelming
compassion, and gracious plans for our
lives. Isn't it wonderful to serve an all-
powerful God who invites us to belong to
Him and live as His beloved daughters now
and forever?

Loving Who God Is

"Let us acknowledge the LORD;
let us press on to acknowledge him."

HOSEA 6:3

Those of us who have ever betrayed our true selves to please someone else know we made a big mistake. That's why God remains God rather than conforming to our notions about Him, or about what He should do for us. In the Bible, God reveals His unconditional love for us, and in creation He displays His creative power. Peace with God comes not from asking Him to be what He isn't, but by loving who He is.

GOD'S WILL

His Good Will

The world and its desire are
passing away, but those who
do the will of God live forever.

1 JOHN 2:17 NRSV

Peace is impossible when our human wills
collide with God's will. Yet unlike a person
who insists on imposing her own will for
selfish reasons, God makes His will known
to us for our benefit. He recognizes where
our talents lie and where our happiness
rests. He sees beyond the present moment
and has determined the best path for our
feet. He never forces His desires on us, but
delights to lead us where His good and gracious will would take us.

Always

*"Stand at the crossroads and look;
ask for the ancient paths, ask where
the good way is, and walk in it, and
you will find rest for your souls."*

JEREMIAH 6:16

God's will for us is not always perfectly
clear. We can imagine Him asking us to
stick with Him a little longer, and perhaps
discover His answer for ourselves as time
passes. Sometimes His answers come in
the unfolding of events, in the "chance"
encounter with a wise and insightful
friend, or in the words of scripture as we
study more deeply and pray more fervently.
God's will is always for us to walk more
closely with Him.

GRATITUDE

Abundance

I will thank the LORD with all my heart.

PSALM 111:1 NCV

Gratitude creates peace, and peace creates gratitude. When we take time out to give thanks for the blessings that we enjoy each day, we realize how much God has given us. And if He has blessed us today, we can trust Him to bless us tomorrow as well. Reliance on Him produces serenity of heart and mind, giving us all the more reason to thank Him again for the abundance of peace we have in Him!

Plenty of Good

Be thankful in all circumstances.

1 Thessalonians 5:18 nlt

It's easy to forget gratitude when face-to-face with trouble, yet gratitude offers unfailing support and help. Gratitude gives us perspective by showing us that, despite the bad, there's still plenty of good around us. It saves us from despair by assuring us that all is not lost, and it instills in us strength to determine our best response and take hold of a productive solution to our problems. A grateful heart is a faithful friend in time of need.

GUILT

His Healing Heart

*I want you to understand what
really matters, so that you may
live pure and blameless lives until
the day of Christ's return.*

PHILIPPIANS 1:10 NLT

For various reasons, we often accept as fact the accusations of others, and we feel responsible for the way they feel. But God does not hold us accountable for the choices others make, only for our own. When our guilt is justified, He is eager to hear our confession and lift its burden from us. When guilt does not belong to us, God strengthens us and helps us lead a hurting soul to His healing heart.

The Only Way to Peace

*"I have swept away your offenses like a cloud, your
sins like the morning mist.
Return to me, for I have redeemed you."*

ISAIAH 44:22

When we have done wrong, guilt keeps
our transgression in front of us. Justifiable
guilt is the tool God uses to draw us toward
Him and the confession of our sin. He
yearns to renew our minds and hearts by
assuring us of His forgiveness. God longs
to restore the bond sin severs between
individuals, and between Himself and us.
Forgiveness, the only way to peace, begins
with a simple, sincere prayer of acknowl-
edgment that, yes, we have sinned.

HONESTY

His Spirit

Happy are those to whom the
Lord imputes no iniquity, and in
whose spirit there is no deceit.

PSALM 32:2 NRSV

Like a pan of simmering water, dishonesty never rests. It keeps us on edge, fearing someone will reveal our deception, our duplicity. God would have us come to Him so He can bathe us in the still, cool waters of His forgiveness. Then, He invites us to allow His Spirit into our hearts. Through His Spirit, we possess the strength, confidence, and courage to live our lives with honesty and integrity.

Authenticity

[Jesus said,] "Whoever can be
trusted with very little can also
be trusted with much, and whoever
is dishonest with very little will
also be dishonest with much."

LUKE 16:10

Being dishonest, even in trivial matters, is like wearing a mask. It hides who we really are and invites others to believe a lie. It even enables us to deceive ourselves. Yet God is never deceived, and He has no desire for us to be deceived by anyone. Whenever dishonesty creeps into our thinking, actions, or relationships, we can turn to Him for the courage and confidence to turn our authentic face to the world.

HOPE

In the Right Place

The Lord is good to those who
hope in him, to those who seek him.

LAMENTATIONS 3:25 NCV

Sometimes we reach the sad realization that we have put our hope in the wrong place. During such times, we appreciate even more the hope God extends to us through the life, death, and resurrection of Jesus. Through His Son, God demonstrated His desire to heal us, forgive us, renew us, and grant us eternal life with Him in heaven. When we put our hope in Him, our hope is in the right place now and forever.

Hope of Heaven

Things that are seen don't last forever,
but things that are not seen are eternal.
That's why we keep our minds on the
things that cannot be seen.

2 CORINTHIANS 4:18 CEV

You may say, "I hope so!" when the outcome is iffy. Yet the hope God holds out for
us is strengthened with His truth and se-
cured with His promises. There's nothing
iffy about it! Our hope of heaven, though
not yet apparent to our physical eyes, is
sure because God is faithful and does what
He says He will do. We may not know all the
particulars, but we don't need to when our
hope rests in Him.

HUMILITY

Humble Hearts

Good and upright is the Lord; therefore
he instructs sinners in the way.
He leads the humble in what is right,
and teaches the humble his way.

PSALM 25:8–9 NRSV

The humility God desires stems from a heart flowing with His love for people. God sent His Son—who died and rose again to show us His love—to bring every soul to Himself, something not one of us could do on our own. Although we have no cause to boast, we do have every reason to see ourselves as beloved daughters of God, of infinite worth in our heavenly Father's sight. As such, our humble hearts look to Him and give thanks!

Gift of Humility

Humble yourselves before the Lord,
and he will lift you up.

JAMES 4:10 GNT

Humility never asks us to deny our accomplishments or run from earned praise. Rather, it simply invites us to remember from whom our gifts, talents, intellect, achievements, and opportunities come. It leads us to feel good when God uses us to inspire and motivate others and when our work makes a difference in the world. A heart blessed with the gift of humility is as close as a prayer, freely available to every one who asks.

ILLNESS

Lift Us Up

Peace of mind makes the body healthy.

PROVERBS 14:30 GNT

Sickness attacks our bodies and weighs down our hearts. But no matter how low we feel, God's presence is there to lift us up. Perhaps even more clearly than when we're in great health, we hear His words of comfort and sense His touch of consolation and renewal. The Great Physician desires to reveal Himself to us in these trying times so we will know that His peace is ours, His love is real, all the time.

Rooted in Love

*You must be compassionate, just as
your Father is compassionate.*

LUKE 6:36 NLT

When infirmity of body, intellect, or
spirit strikes a loved one, we're often
at a loss, not knowing what to say or do.
Yet those who suffer need us the most!
When we thoughtfully consider how we
would like to be treated under the same
circumstances, how to respond to others
becomes clear. It's a response rooted in
love and compassion, giving us the peace of
knowing that we have done the right thing.

INDECISION

Visit with Him

Trust in the LORD with all your heart,
and lean not on your own understanding; in all
your ways acknowledge Him,
and He shall direct your paths.

PROVERBS 3:5–6 NKJV

God cares about the decisions we make, both big and small. He invites us to come to Him when we don't know which way to turn and let Him point us in the right direction. His response may come in the whisper of our intuition, the stirring of our feelings, the conviction of our hearts, or the voice of a wise friend or counselor. Often, our indecision is God's invitation to visit with Him, to tell Him what's on our minds.

Life Decisions

*Whether you turn to the right
or to the left, your ears will
hear a voice behind you, saying,
"This is the way; walk in it."*

ISAIAH 30:21

A commitment to God's principles turns major life decisions into no-brainers! No, we're not going to think, do, or say what God has forbidden; and yes, we are going to think, do, and say what He has commanded. The opinions of others and even our own feelings fail to upset us, because our Spirit-schooled hearts have already chosen the path they will take. Meanwhile, we can concentrate on life's other choices, like which shoes we'll wear today!

INTOLERANCE

Pardon

*Love one another
deeply from the heart.*

1 PETER 1:22 NRSV

Intolerance has two victims: one, the
target of mean-spirited thinking and
stereotyping; and two, the heart that
harbors it. God works to bring peace
to both sides: He embraces victims of
intolerance with the spirit of forgiveness so
they may pardon others as their heavenly
Father has forgiven them; and He stirs the
feelings of perpetrators so they are led to
seek peace with God by loving others with
the unconditional, accepting love God has
for everyone.

A Loving Invitation

Love is patient, love is kind.

1 CORINTHIANS 13:4

When we uphold God's moral law, we may be labeled "intolerant" by those who wish to follow their own desires. Yet our godly intolerance is not aimed at individuals, but at behavior God has called wrong and conduct outside His will for people. Our goal is not to judge others (God will take care of that), but to lovingly invite them to reach out to the God of forgiveness, compassion, and love, because His arms are reaching out to them.

Contentment

*It is better to be content with
what little you have. Otherwise,
you will always be struggling for more,
and that is like chasing the wind.*

ECCLESIASTES 4:6 NCV

As we more fully embrace God's will for our lives and accept His wisdom in all things concerning us, jealousy becomes less and less of a threat to our inner peace. There's no room in our hearts for envy, because our hearts overflow with gratitude for everything God has given to us. We cannot imagine coveting the life or possessions of another, because we rest content in the privilege of being who we are, beloved daughters of God.

Our Worship

*"You must worship no other gods,
for the LORD, whose very name is
Jealous, is a God who is jealous
about his relationship with you."*

EXODUS 34:14 NLT

It's hard to think of God as being jealous, isn't it? He is, and in all the right ways! As our Creator and Lord, God is justifiably jealous of any person or thing we might revere in His place. He knows our security lies in no other name but His, and He sees the destructive path ahead for those who follow false gods. That's why God demands our worship—not because *He* needs it, but because He knows *we* do.

LEADERSHIP

Our Eternal Leader

*[Jesus said,] "Whoever wants to be a
leader among you must be your servant."*

MATTHEW 20:26 NLT

Whether we have looked forward to a
leadership position, or it was thrust upon
us, we now bear its many responsibilities.
But as long as we follow God, our eternal
leader, our headship will serve to bless
those under our direction. His leadership
shields us from the pitfalls of pride and the
misuse of power. His way opens our hearts
to forgive those who may criticize us un-
fairly, and embraces us with His wisdom,
strength, and confidence.

Spiritual Leaders

*Be an example to all believers in
what you say, in the way you live,
in your love, your faith, and your purity.*

1 TIMOTHY 4:12 NLT

As women who follow God, we are spiritual leaders. God, through the work of the Holy Spirit evident in the things we do and say, gives us the privilege of guiding others to Him by our example. Our willingness to forgive leads others in the way of forgiveness, and our genuine happiness, true contentment, and inner peace influence others more than we'll ever know. More than ever, we must follow God, and lead with genuine joy!

LIFE'S PURPOSE

Serve Him Best

*The Lord will fulfill his purpose
for me; your steadfast love, O Lord,
endures forever. Do not forsake
the work of your hands.*

PSALM 138:8 NRSV

After years, perhaps decades, of going about life our own way, we conclude that life is meaningless. That's the predictable outcome when we fail to recognize God as our creator who has given us rules to keep us safe, resources to use for good, and blessings to enjoy and share. Our life's purpose emerges as we let Him lead according to His will and wisdom, because He alone knows where and how we can serve Him best.

Our Life's Diary

"Who knows but that you have
come to your royal position
for such a time as this?"

ESTHER 4:14

For those of us who kept a diary when we were young, we may have filled many pages with passing thoughts and seemingly insignificant notes. But, looking back, we realize how God was preparing us to become the women we are today. The things we experienced, endured, and encountered fit into God's purpose for our lives. He's not finished with our life's "diary" yet, but when He is, we will have reason to rejoice with Him forever.

LONELINESS

Banishing Loneliness

I am always with you;
you hold me by my right hand.

PSALM 73:23

The ache of loneliness drags us down both physically and emotionally. It saps our energy and burdens our minds with self-doubt and feelings of rejection. God, in His compassion, desires to remove loneliness from our lives by assuring us of His unshakeable, unconquerable love for us. His Spirit, alive in our hearts, reminds us of His presence, offering us the power to banish loneliness and bathe in the tranquility of His devotion and faithfulness to us.

Continuing Relationship

We are many parts of one body,
and we all belong to each other.

ROMANS 12:5 NLT

A sudden life change can throw even the most outgoing person into the throes of loneliness. That's why God may invite us to step forward and reach out to our friends and loved ones who are trying to cope with new circumstances. Our willingness to quietly listen, gently encourage, and kindly guide reflects the way God responds to us whenever we feel lonely. It's His way of nurturing our continuing relationship with Him and with others.

LOSS

Hope for Tomorrow

*He comforts us every time we have
trouble, so when others have trouble,
we can comfort them with the
same comfort God gives us.*

2 CORINTHIANS 1:4 NCV

Loss hurts, and it's important for us to recognize our pain and open ourselves to God's comfort and to the consolation of others. While nothing can take the place of what has been lost, the promises of God offer us hope for tomorrow, and the presence of friends and loved ones supports us in our grief. We were never meant to bear loss alone, but to walk hand in hand through sorrow, with our footsteps following His will and purpose.

Something to Cheer About

You have given up your old way
of life with its habits. Each of
you is now a new person.

COLOSSIANS 3:9–10 CEV

Hooray for loss when we're talking about destructive behavior, excess weight, or habitual sin! Yet even these losses leave an empty space in our lives, and it's into these spaces that God wishes to enter. Through the power of His Spirit working to change our lives for the better, our loss becomes our gain in self-confidence, satisfaction, and happiness. It's something to cheer about, giving thanks to God, who richly fills our every need.

MARRIAGE

God's Intention

Let all that you do be done in love.

1 CORINTHIANS 16:14, NRSV

Mutual fulfillment, friendship, faithfulness—these describe God's intention for marriage. Yet the perfect marriage doesn't exist because we are not perfect people. God asks us to come to Him without shame when things go wrong in marriage, because He knows our weaknesses and everything we're feeling and experiencing. In Him, we find peace in forgiving and in being forgiven, and the wisdom to resolve our problems according to His will and guidance.

Firm Foundation

Give honor to marriage, and remain
faithful to one another in marriage.

HEBREWS 13:4 NLT

When newly married, a husband and wife are tempted to make their love the center of their life together. God, however, has another suggestion. He offers Himself as the center of marriage, because He never changes, never disappoints, and always loves. He is ready to listen and understand, and to strengthen, build up, and make new. God, who has blessed us with the gift of marriage, is willing and able to stand as its strong support and firm foundation.

MATERIALISM

Thankful for Blessings

Jesus said to them, "Be careful and guard against all kinds of greed. Life is not measured by how much one owns."

LUKE 12:15 NCV

The recent economic recession has highlighted an important truth. We saw what happens when, instead of worshipping the God who gives us possessions, we worship the possessions. For this sin, as for all others, God sent His Son, Jesus, to win our forgiveness. During His earthly ministry, Jesus showed us how to live as spiritual beings in a material world, contented with what we have, thankful for our blessings, and eager to share with those in need.

Sharing

Honor the LORD with your wealth,
with the firstfruits of all your crops; then your
barns will be filled to overflowing, and your vats
will brim over with new wine.

PROVERBS 3:9–10

Our God-sent material possessions serve to bless our lives with comfort and pleasure. In addition, they provide us with the privilege of blessing the lives of those who have less than we do, sharing with them as God shares with us. We live peacefully and at ease in our world of abundance when we neither covet nor grasp at possessions, but use whatever we have to the glory of God, giving Him thanks and praise.

MISCARRIAGE

With Open Arms

Out of the depths have I cried unto thee,
O Lord. Lord, hear my voice: let thine ears be
attentive to the voice of my supplications.

PSALM 130:1–2 KJV

The pain of a miscarriage strikes not only the body but also the heart and soul. There, even in the darkest shadows of our sorrow, stands our God. With open arms, He longs to enfold us in His compassionate love. He won't try to soothe us with answers because no explanation could possibly set our minds at rest. His strong and steady presence is the only thing powerful enough to see us through to the light of another dawn.

He Won't Forget

It is good for me to be near you.
I choose you as my protector.

PSALM 73:28 CEV

Even if it happened years ago, a woman never forgets the loss of her unborn child—and she doesn't want to. She knows God asks her to trust His wisdom, but it's tough to do when the little life growing inside her has been lost. God knows the tears we shed at each *if only* that goes through our minds, and He understands the emptiness we feel, no matter how much time goes by. He'll never forget—and He doesn't want to.

MISJUDGMENT

First Impressions

The heart of the godly thinks carefully before speaking.

PROVERBS 15:28 NLT

First impressions are powerful, but they're often wrong. The first thing we notice about a person or hear about an event certainly isn't the whole story. Only when we're open to suspending judgment, to welcoming further information, and to allowing more time for observation can we avoid the error of misjudgment. First impressions are intense, impatient to have their way, but the wisest among us will calmly wait until first impressions have given way to facts.

As He Is

Grow in grace, and in the knowledge
of our Lord and Saviour Jesus Christ.

2 PETER 3:18 KJV

When we have sinned, we might avoid God because we think He will punish us. If we believe ourselves unlovable, we may be drawn to think He couldn't possibly love us as we are. These misjudgments stand between us and the God who overflows with kindness and forgiveness, compassion and gentleness. Try Him, test Him, and see if these things are true. Doing so will bring us the peace of knowing our heavenly Father as He truly is.

MISTAKES

Make Amends

*As far as the east is from the west,
so far has [God] removed our
transgressions from us.*

PSALM 103:12 NKJV

How we hate to make mistakes! But now
is the time to step back, own up to our actions, and make amends where possible.
Then we can step forward, leaving the mistake far behind. Because Jesus has brought
us into relationship with our heavenly
Father, that's the way God treats our sins:
After we've confessed and received His
pardon, He puts the sin behind us, urging
us to continue our journey as cleansed, forgiven, and beloved women of God.

Everything Will Be Okay

*Everyone has sinned and is far away
from God's saving presence. But by
the free gift of God's grace all are put right
with him through Christ Jesus.*

ROMANS 3:23–24 GNT

All of us make mistakes, but God never does. In fact, He has the power to turn our mistakes around, so even those things we have badly botched end up working for our good. Humble admission of our guilt and unconditional faith in His forgiveness through Jesus Christ gets God working on our behalf, and when He's in charge, we can take a deep breath and relax, knowing everything will turn out okay in the end.

MONEY MATTERS

Financial Resources

You cannot serve both God and money.

LUKE 16:13 GNT

Few issues cause more anxiety than those concerning money. The stress begins when we forget that money is a resource provided by God, not a substitute for Him. He willingly gives us what He knows is best for us and, guided by His Spirit, we manage our financial resources wisely and well. There's nothing to worry about, because our security rests with the giver, not the gift. Our spirit finds peace in Him alone.

Rely on Him

*"Lay up for yourselves
treasures in heaven."*

MATTHEW 6:20 NKJV

During His earthly ministry, Jesus shared with all who would listen, then and now, about greed, discontent, and indebtedness—the unsettling consequences of a wrong relationship with money. He urges us to rely on Him to provide, because He knows how much money we need and why we need it. When our relationship with Him stands on unwavering trust in His faithfulness, our relationship with money rests easy in our hearts and minds.

MORALITY

God's Commandments

Don't be immoral in matters of sex.
That is a sin against your own body
in a way that no other sin is.

1 CORINTHIANS 6:18 CEV

At a certain age, we might avoid looking in a mirror under a strong light! Even more uncomfortable, however, is examining our lifestyle under the glare of God's commandments. Where the blemish of immorality or the wrinkle of sin exists, God yearns to renew us with His full pardon, earned for us by His Son, Jesus. Through the power of His Spirit, He restores us to Himself as flawless and holy, completely beautiful in His sight.

The Reason

Your hands have made me and fashioned me;
give me understanding, that I
may learn Your commandments.

PSALM 119:73 NKJV

God treats us as His beloved daughters,
and He has no wish to keep us away from
what will make us truly happy. When our
desires clash with His commandments, we
find our peace in knowing He's keeping
us safe in body and spirit. We rest in the
arms of one who can see the sad end of the
world's careless ways. When God says no,
He says it for a reason, and the reason is
love.

MOTIVATION

The Fullness of His Spirit

You want me to be completely truthful,
so teach me wisdom.

PSALM 51:6 NCV

When something we did appears all right but leaves us feeling uneasy, God may be prompting us to question our motivation. Even better than we can ourselves, God can read our hearts. If He finds self-interest, lust, or hostility hidden there, He desires to draw it out so we can enjoy the fullness of His Spirit dwelling within us. With the assurance of His pardon, we can confidently confide even our deepest motivations in His presence.

The Drive

Whatever you do, work at it
with all your heart, as though
you were working for the
Lord and not for people.

COLOSSIANS 3:23 GNT

What motivates us matters. That's why
God calls us to complete obedience to Him
and loving service to others as our motivation in all things. It's why we get up in the
morning, and it's the drive behind our
thoughts, actions, and decisions. It's how
we can go to bed at night in peace, because
no matter where the day took us, we did everything to the best of our ability and to the
glory of God and our neighbor.

OBEDIENCE

God's Rules

This is the love of God, that we keep his commandments: and his commandments are not grievous.

1 JOHN 5:3 KJV

On the books of countless communities and organizations are outdated, irrelevant rules. The same *cannot* be said of the rules governing morality that God has set down in His book, the Bible. Because the human heart has not changed with time, God's rules apply to us as surely as they did to His people of ages past. Then as now, willing and joyful obedience in the things we think, say, and do every day brings us closer to God.

The Fence of Freedom

If you look carefully into the perfect law that sets
you free, and if you do what it says. . .then God
will bless you for doing it.

JAMES 1:25 NLT

Like a fence that protects a beautiful gar-
den, God sets around us the barrier of His
standards. This allows us to enjoy our lives
and our relationships within the bounds
of God's good intentions for us, and it
protects us from destructive habits, atti-
tudes, and behaviors. We can look at God's
standards as a fence of freedom. Because it
keeps us away from sin, we are free to grow
abundantly in peace, love, and happiness.

THE PAST

Dissolve the Darkness

The world will make you suffer.
But be brave! I have defeated the world!

JOHN 16:33 GNT

Like a shadow, a troubled past can darken
the present with disturbing thoughts and
distressing memories. God, who was there
with us, knows what happened; and even
more, He knows why He permitted it to
happen. We can pour out our pain to Him,
hiding none of our feelings. Then allow
Him to dissolve the darkness with the light
of His healing touch and lift the gloom
of painful memories. "Why?" is His; but
peace is ours.

A New Course

Understanding your word brings
light to the minds of ordinary people.

PSALM 119:130 CEV

We wish things had been different, but they weren't. Now what? Though we cannot remake the past, God has given us today to decide on a new course, to lay a fresh foundation. This time, we know to take Him into our confidence as we think about our future and plan how to get there. This time, even if we need to work a little harder, we will make it, because our strong advocate is also our support and guide.

PERFECTIONISM

The Perfect Answer

*You will keep in perfect peace
all who trust in you, all whose
thoughts are fixed on you!*

ISAIAH 26:3 NLT

Most of us have an impression of an ideal woman that glows in our mind's eye. But in most cases, we're frustrated for we have yet to reach her level of perfection. Our God reaches out to us with a smile, because He yearns to relieve us of the burden of perfectionism. He adores the women we really are—windblown hair, smudged mascara, chipped fingernails, and all! Let's allow Him to free us to love the women we really are, and in doing so, wrap ourselves up in His wonderful peace. God is the perfect answer to perfectionism.

His Perfection

By one sacrifice [Jesus Christ]
has made perfect forever those
who are being made holy.

HEBREWS 10:14

The only perfect, sinless person to walk among us was Jesus Christ. Through His acts of healing, kindness, and mercy, He set an example for us to follow. Our Lord begs us not to burden ourselves by grasping at our concept of perfection, or suffering because of the flaws we see around us. Christ's genuine perfection is ours to receive. It is His perfection that we possess through faith in His life, death, and resurrection.

PERSEVERANCE

Together

"I will never leave you nor forsake you."

JOSHUA 1:5

At one time or another, most of us have prayed for God to get us out of a tough situation. But He didn't. Why? Because it's possible His hand was outstretched for ours so that the two of us could walk through it together. With Him, we have an infinite source of support, power, strength, and wisdom in any and all situations. As His daughters, we possess the promise of His presence wherever the path may lead, and the assurance of triumph, because our victory rests in Him.

Willingness to Persevere

Let endurance have its full effect,
so that you may be mature and
complete, lacking in nothing.

JAMES 1:4 NRSV

The way of faith isn't always calm. Disquieting times of spiritual apathy, dryness, doubt, and even persecution make us wonder if it's all worth it. God may send these kinds of tests our way, because we need to discover the strength of our commitment to Him. Our willingness to persevere in prayer, meditation, and Bible study affirms us as we find more and more peace, joy, and confidence as women of God.

PRAYER

The Whisper of His Spirit

*Continue in prayer, and watch
in the same with thanksgiving.*

COLOSSIANS 4:2 KJV

It isn't difficult to understand why at times we feel awkward praying. After all, how do we know we're not chattering into thin air? But even in our doubt, God encourages us to pour out our deepest thoughts to Him and then to listen. We stop speaking and wait for the whisper of His Spirit to enter our consciousness. Then we hear Him assure us of His presence and gently invite us to continue our conversation with Him.

The Sweet Sound

What other nation is so great as to have their gods near them the way the Lord our God is near us whenever we pray to him?

DEUTERONOMY 4:7

When we pray, do we kneel or stand? Do we speak in words that have echoed through the ages, or in the spontaneous utterances of our own hearts? Do we hold our thoughts for a private time with Him, or speak to Him in the workplace or as we go about our daily activities? Let none of these things disturb us however, whenever, or wherever we pray. Because God is interested in only one thing: the sweet sound of our voices.

PREGNANCY

Surrender

I will trust, and will not be afraid,
for the Lord God is my strength and
my might; he has become my salvation.

Isaiah 12:2 NRSV

Maybe it's not what we expected, at least not now. The feelings of anxiety, apprehension, and even anger that course through our hearts and minds are natural, and they're feelings we can take to God. Without fearing His disapproval, we can tell Him everything. Then we, along with the new life growing inside us, can walk into His embrace, there to surrender ourselves to His loving arms and yield to the unexpected changes in our plans. Peace comes when we let the coming months draw us ever closer to Him, our ever-present comfort and help.

Support and Strength

Unto you that fear my name
shall the Sun of righteousness
arise with healing in his wings.

MALACHI 4:2 KJV

We're nothing like the beaming mother-to-be on the magazine cover. Our roller-coaster emotions and aching backs tell a whole different story! But our Great Physician is always there, inviting us to remember His compassion and love as we entrust our health and well-being to Him. We can ask Him for the support we need, and receive it in abundance through the strength He gives us and the help He provides through the hearts and hands of others.

PRIDE

Who We Really Are

*Be honest in your evaluation of
yourselves, measuring yourselves
by the faith God has given us.*

ROMANS 12:3 NLT

While our pride suggests that the problem rests with others, God's Spirit tells the truth. He does this not to condemn us, but to draw us to the knowledge of who we really are. In Him, we have no need to set ourselves above others or envy their praise and applause. While He reaches down to us with His peace, we receive the joy of reaching across to others as beloved sisters and brothers in the family of God.

Humility and Self-Respect

When pride comes, then comes disgrace,
but with humility comes wisdom.

PROVERBS 11:2

Healthy pride gives us the ability to stand tall, but unhealthy pride makes us think we tower over others. All our relationships suffer, including our relationship with God. That's why He urges us to let Him root out self-importance wherever it lurks, replacing it with genuine humility and godly self-respect. Then we can take our rightful place with and among others, our relationships marked by generosity, peace, mutual support, encouragement, and delight.

PRINCIPLES

Inner Peace

We remember before our God and Father
your work produced by faith, your labor
prompted by love, and your endurance
inspired by hope in our Lord Jesus Christ.

1 THESSALONIANS 1:3

Sometimes sticking to biblical principles brings not peace but friction. Yet the friction exists only on the outside, because inside, we're standing on the firm foundation of God's commandments. Our inner peace depends not on the applause of friends and loved ones who have chosen another way, but on the approval of God, who has our safety, security, and spiritual prosperity at heart. He is the source of lasting peace!

His Principles

The fruit of the Spirit is love,
joy, peace, forbearance, kindness, goodness,
faithfulness, gentleness
and self-control. Against such
things there is no law.

GALATIANS 5:22–23

If we desire peace, the God of peace draws us to live by His principles. His commandments are designed to guide us along His path so that we can avoid the pitfalls of sin. His Spirit works within us to keep our hearts and minds in Him and away from the conflicts of envy, greed, and arrogance. God's Son, Jesus, holds out to us a right relationship with Him, one marked by faith, trust, and love. By following His principles, peace is yours.

PRIORITIES

What Comes First

*"Seek first God's kingdom and
what God wants. Then all your
other needs will be met as well."*

MATTHEW 6:33 NCV

If all we need to do each day leaves us
drained and discouraged, it's time to talk
with God about our priorities. He invites us
to put Him first in mind, heart, and action;
and then He promises us that everything
else will fall into place. When His priorities
guide our decisions, it's easy to separate real
responsibilities from those things that steal
our time and energy. No more frustration!
Only the peace and pleasure of knowing
what comes first.

What Really Matters

*"Choose this day whom you will serve. . .
but as for me and my household,
we will serve the Lord."*

JOSHUA 24:15 NRSV

If God sets our priorities, we know what's truly important. We're able to resist the pull of selfish impulses and empty distractions. We receive His Spirit to guide us toward lasting goals, such as love for God and others, and we have His perspective on where our time and attention is best directed. At the end of the day, we lie down fulfilled and satisfied because we've thought, said, and done those things that really matter.

PROVOCATION

A New Response

Don't become angry quickly,
because getting angry is foolish.

ECCLESIASTES 7:9 NCV

Someone knows all the right buttons
to push! While we're tempted to react in
kind, we know our anger will only escalate
the argument. God's way offers us a new
response, a response that might never
change our tormentor, but will certainly
change us. His way strengthens us to meet
provocation with His Spirit of patience and
kindness, forgiveness and love. With Him,
our peace is assured. And who knows? It
might rub off on you-know-who!

Power to Bring Peace

*[Love] keeps no record
of being wronged.*

1 CORINTHIANS 13:5 NLT

God is love, but He hates sin. Sin, incompatible with His holiness, provokes Him to rightful anger, but then His love steps in. Out of love, His Son, Jesus, faced God's anger for us by winning our complete forgiveness through His life, death, and resurrection. With His Spirit alive in our hearts, we, too, meet provocation with patience. We, too, hate provocative behavior but love the person. We, too, have the power to bring peace.

REBELLION

Caring Counselor

*Let the wicked. . .turn to the Lord that he may
have mercy on them. Yes, turn to our God,
for he will forgive generously.*

ISAIAH 55:7 NLT

In the course of growing up, many of us
went through a stage of rebellion. Often
under the guidance of a parent or teacher,
however, we matured, and our troubled
spirits found peace. Whenever we take a
stand against God, He reveals Himself to
us as our compassionate Father and caring
Counselor. He has no interest in punishing
us, but in entering our hearts and minds so
we can continue growing in spiritual maturity, holiness, and grace.

Change of Heart

I will cleanse them from all the guilt of their sin
against me, and I will forgive all the guilt of their
sin and rebellion against me.

JEREMIAH 33:8 NRSV

When a loved one rebels against our
godly principles and values, we hurt. We
hurt for the person who stubbornly clings
to a destructive lifestyle, and we hurt for
ourselves because we had higher hopes and
expectations. Our prayers to God go to one
who shares our hurt and understands what
rebellion against good feels like. As we
pray, we can find our comfort in believing
that forgiveness is available and a change of
heart possible for every erring soul.

REGRET

Genuine Peace

The Lord has made a solemn promise,
and he will not abandon you, for he has
decided to make you his own people.

1 SAMUEL 12:22 GNT

We make many decisions, some of which we later regret. While healthy regret probes our thinking and motivation so we don't make the same mistake again, unhealthy regret stirs up anguish of heart and mind, often still potent years after the event. Our prayers to God for help with regret permits Him to lift its onerous burden and draw us to genuine acceptance. Acceptance stands as His bridge between unhealthy regret and genuine peace.

Renew and Restore

Godly sorrow brings repentance that leads to salvation and leaves no regret.

2 CORINTHIANS 7:10

Now that we're faced with the consequences, we wish we could go back and undo everything! But God restricts us to this time and this place. Genuine regret over past mistakes has the power to bring us to God today, and it's here and now that He extends His hands in forgiveness. As He pardons us, He offers to guide us through our unhappy circumstances, for He has the desire to renew and restore His peace to the humble, repentant heart.

RELATIONSHIPS

Centered in God's Love

*Peacemakers who sow in peace
reap a harvest of righteousness.*

JAMES 3:18

When an argument flares between us and a friend or loved one, our stress level skyrockets. We can take steps to restore harmony by asking God to help us pinpoint the real problem. His perspective lets us differentiate simple misunderstandings from complex issues, and His guidance works toward healing for us and the others involved. Relationships are worth the work it takes to keep them strong—and our prayers to keep them centered in God's love.

Day or Night

[Jesus said,] "I stand at the door and knock.
If you hear my voice and open the door,
I will come in and eat with you."

REVELATION 3:20 NCV

No earthy relationship thrives without effort on our part to keep it healthy, lively, and strong. Our relationship with Jesus Christ is no different. While He has initiated the relationship, our Spirit-prompted response transforms it into a meaningful and significant part of our lives. Christ's presence, like that of a faithful friend, is something we can rely on. He is someone we can call on, day or night. It's the relationship of a lifetime—and beyond.

REPUTATION

Building Blocks

*People. . .might say that you are
doing wrong. Live such good lives
that they will see the good things
you do and will give glory to God.*

1 PETER 2:12 NCV

Perhaps the good name we carry has suffered because of some past behavior or malicious tale passed around by others. Whatever the case, God's principles are the building blocks that can help us regain what has been lost. Our day-to-day obedience to Him reveals the lie behind false rumors and shows everyone who knows us the kind of person we really are. We won't need to worry about what we did or what others say; our God-guided actions will tell our new and true story.

Women of God

We are careful to be honorable before the Lord,
but we also want everyone else to see
that we are honorable.

2 CORINTHIANS 8:21 NLT

The reputation we carry as women of good
character is worth keeping. It contributes
to our emotional well-being, our ability
to make friends with other people of
godly character, and our eligibility for
responsible positions in church, business,
and the community. Even more important,
however, is the reputation we carry as
women of God. It's a reputation gained
among others when they see our spiritual
commitment carried out in words and
actions of kindness and love.

RESPONSIBILITIES

Downtime

*Thus said the Lord God, the Holy
One of Israel: In returning and
rest you shall be saved; in quietness
and in trust shall be your strength.*

ISAIAH 30:15 NRSV

Sometimes we're so busy meeting the
demands of others that we have little or
no downtime. While it's good and God-
pleasing to carry out our responsibilities
each day, there's a danger when outside
demands threaten our inner peace. Jesus,
in His earthly ministry, took time out from
His teaching and preaching to pray to His
heavenly Father. In doing so, He set an example that applies today, especially when
we feel burdened with way too much to do.

Votes of Confidence

We must try to become mature and start
thinking about more than just the basic
things we were taught about Christ.

HEBREWS 6:1 CEV

Because she has confidence in her, a mother gives her daughter greater responsibilities. Similarly, God grants us increasing responsibilities as we mature spiritually and learn how to put His will into practice. From our responsibility to God to thank and praise Him, to our responsibility to others to love and care for them, God's Spirit gives us the privilege of taking on more and more. We should rejoice in the many votes of confidence our God has given us!

RISK

In Faith and Confidence

If any of you is lacking in wisdom,
ask God, who gives to all generously and
ungrudgingly, and it will be given you.

JAMES 1:5 NRSV

Action involves risk, and many of us are
uncomfortable with risk. But if we never
take action, we certainly will lose opportunities, bypass relationships, and block the
way to a joyful, satisfying life. God helps us
handle risk by giving us the power to reason, weigh pros and cons, and consult with
others as well as God, and then to step forward in faith and confidence when we have
reached our best decision. And whatever
the outcome, He will be there with us.

Certainty

Unto thee, O LORD, do I lift up my soul.
O my God, I trust in thee:
let me not be ashamed.

PSALM 25:1–2 KJV

There are risks involved in loving God. We risk having to say no to desires that are contrary to God's will for us. We risk the ridicule of those who prefer their own perspective to God's wisdom, and we risk times of trial and testing. But here's where certainty steps in: By trusting in and loving Him, we gain a purposeful and meaningful life as a spiritually mature woman of God, able to receive His blessings with pure gladness and experience His peace with unfettered joy.

SACRIFICE

Expressions of Love

*"I tell you the truth, anything
you did for even the least of my
people here, you also did for me."*

MATTHEW 25:40 NCV

A sacrifice is a choice made for a higher
good. We sacrifice our resources to share
with our loved ones, and we sacrifice our
time to help someone in need. While we
might grumble occasionally at the sacri-
fices we make, God's Spirit moves us to see
them as expressions of love, for that's what
they are. More than a lifetime of grasping
to get what we want, sacrificing to serve
others brings meaning to life and heart-
deep fulfillment and joy.

Nurturing

*Christ is the sacrifice that takes away our sins
and the sins of all the world's people.*

1 JOHN 2:2 CEV

If we love someone, we nurture the
relationship. We might even sacrifice our
own desires simply to make our loved one
happy. Because of love, Jesus sacrificed
His life on the cross to establish our
relationship with His heavenly Father.
Christ's death and resurrection show how
far God will go to call us into relationship
and keep us in there with Him. We should
take pleasure in our relationship with Him
because He nurtures it with His love.

SCRIPTURES

"Yes!"

*Everything that was written in the past
was written to teach us. The Scriptures
give us patience and encouragement so
that we can have hope.*

ROMANS 15:4, NCV

At the beginning of a romantic relationship, we might wonder if a man's feelings for us are as strong as ours are for him. In our relationship with God, however, we have our answer right away. God has revealed His attitude toward us in the words of scripture so we never have to wonder if He loves us, or guess whether He listens to our prayers. His "Yes!" rings throughout scripture, because He wants us to live with certainty of His love, peace, and protection.

Glowing with Good Health

Your word is a lamp to my
feet and a light to my path.

PSALM 119:105 NRSV

Daily scripture reading is like maintaining a healthy diet. We may not remember every one of our meals, yet we're healthier because of them. When we read and meditate on the Bible, God's words to us, the Holy Spirit strengthens our faith and nourishes us with a deeper understanding of God's will for our lives. We may not remember everything we read (or even what we read this morning!), but our hearts and souls will glow with good health.

SELF-AWARENESS

Redeemed and Beloved

*God loved us so much that he made
us alive with Christ, and God's
wonderful kindness is what saves you.*

EPHESIANS 2:4–5 CEV

Know yourself." In the Bible, God describes how He wants us to think, speak, and act so we will realize we cannot live up to His desires. At the same time, God expresses His love for us and outlines His plan of salvation for us so we're able to see ourselves as redeemed and beloved women of God. When we know ourselves as God knows us, we can live at peace with Him, with others, and with ourselves.

Whose We Are

*Thank you for making me so
wonderfully complex! Your workmanship
is marvelous—how well I know it.*

PSALM 139:14, NLT

Self-awareness requires us to recognize
our weaknesses and invites us to thank God
for our strengths. When we celebrate our
unique God-given strengths by naming
them, developing them, and using them for
our good and the good of others, we begin
to see ourselves as gifted, talented, and capable women. Our confidence grows as our
self-awareness deepens, centered in knowing who we are and, even more importantly,
whose we are.

SERVICE

Serving Others

"Anyone who wants to be my disciple must follow me, because my servants must be where I am. And the Father will honor anyone who serves me."

JOHN 12:26 NLT

No matter where we are in life, God grants us the privilege of serving Him by serving others. As we embrace God's principle of sharing as our own, we come to experience life in a whole new way. As we follow the Holy Spirit's promptings in choosing our life's direction, we discover life's purpose. Others may not understand why we have set our sights on service, but we will as we experience genuine joy and heart-deep peace.

God Serves

*There are different ways
to serve the same Lord.*

1 CORINTHIANS 12:5 CEV

As God serves us, we serve others. If we're in a humble position, we serve by taking genuine pleasure in our ability to help, assist, cheer, and encourage others. If we're in an influential position, we serve by speaking and acting on behalf of others, promoting fairness for all, and living as an example for others to follow. But service doesn't always come easy, and that's why God serves us each day with His wisdom, strength, and love.

SINGLENESS

A Special Ministry

*A woman who is no longer married
or has never been married can be devoted
to the Lord and holy in body and in spirit.*

1 CORINTHIANS 7:34, NLT

Just as God wishes to take His place within marriage, so He desires to dwell within singleness. He invites those of us who are single to enjoy the fullness of life by directing our attention to the needs of others, and He leads our heart to places where we can make a difference for the good. Singleness, whether for a time or for a lifetime, is a special ministry granted by God for His purposes. Live it in confidence, in joy, and in peace!

Peace in Singleness

Since you are God's people, it is
not right that any matters of sexual
immorality or indecency or greed
should even be mentioned among you.

EPHESIANS 5:3 GNT

Many would dismiss celibacy as an outdated concept, but God doesn't. To single people, God still requires purity of mind and body. He knows how challenging this can be, but He also knows that when our single lifestyle "marries" His standards— by saying no to the promptings of our flesh and the lures of our culture—we are honoring our Spirit-strengthened vow. Our peace in singleness comes through a lifestyle devoted to others and their needs, and to God and His holiness.

SPEECH

Power of Words

Gracious words are a honeycomb,
sweet to the soul and healing to the bones.

PROVERBS 16:24

For most of us, speaking comes easy. So easy, in fact, that we forget the power of the words we use when talking to others. Just as words can convey love, kindness, care, and compassion, they can also provoke anger, cause hurt feelings, and bring offense. God's Spirit working in us prompts us to choose our words with their power in mind, using them to give thanks to God and bless the lives of others.

His Name

*"Good people have good things
in their hearts, and so they
say good things."*

MATTHEW 12:35 NCV

If we were to hear a loved one insulted, we'd feel justifiably angry. Yet when we use God's name frivolously and uselessly, we insult His Spirit dwelling within us. The twinge of guilt or nervous laughter that follows reminds us that we love God and respect His name and His holiness. No matter how often we hear it or who uses it, profanity has no place in our speech as God's beloved, forgiven, and gentle-tongued women.

SPIRITUAL STRUGGLE

Victory

*Thank God for letting our Lord
Jesus Christ give us the victory!*

1 CORINTHIANS 15:57 CEV

We don't associate struggle with peace, but God does. In our spiritual struggle with temptations like doubt, envy, intolerance, impatience, and anger, God reminds us that His Son, Jesus, has won the victory for us. Jesus overcame temptation of all kinds, enabling us to lean on Him during our own battles. With His Spirit at work in our hearts and minds, we struggle, but we already know the outcome. We can do the impossible: struggle against sin, yet remain confident of winning!

Mightier Than Temptation

The temptations in your life are no
different from what others experience.
And God. . .will not allow the temptation to be
more than you can stand.

1 CORINTHIANS 10:13 NLT

The best way to meet temptation is with God's Word. In the Bible, we discover others who have struggled with the same things now burdening us, and we find God's assurance of strength, power, and ultimate victory. His promises support us with wisdom and insight, shield us with Spirit-fed confidence, and build up our faith to withstand the lure of temptation. Receive lasting peace in knowing God is mightier than any temptation to sin.

STARTING OVER

The Way Ahead

"Don't lose your courage or be afraid.
Don't panic or be frightened, because
the LORD your God goes with you."

DEUTERONOMY 20:3–4, NCV

Starting over after misfortune takes
courage, especially when we're not
quite sure how to proceed. Our times of
prayer and meditation take on an added
importance, because we realize that only
God's guiding Spirit can show us the way
ahead. We want to listen and learn. We want
to do the right thing, and just knowing He
is there gives us the fortitude we need to
confidently enter this new chapter of our
lives.

Back on the Path

*Create in me a pure heart, O God, and renew a
steadfast spirit within me.*

Not one of us travels in a straight, smooth
line to spiritual maturity. As long as we
live this side of heaven, we'll stumble, fall
down, and wander into dangerous places.
Then when we realize our mistake and turn
to God for forgiveness, our heavenly Father
rushes in to pick us up, dust us off, and set
us back on our path. Yes, we're stronger
now, and wiser. With a hug and a smile, our
God lets us start over.

SUFFERING

God Knows

*Be glad for the chance to suffer as
Christ suffered. It will prepare you
for even greater happiness when
he makes his glorious return.*

1 PETER 4:13 CEV

When we pour out our hearts to God, we are speaking to one who knows suffering. Our heavenly Father experienced the loss of His Son when Jesus died on the cross, and Jesus suffered injustice, mistreatment, and condemnation. God the Holy Spirit suffers when souls fall into sin and refuse His rescue. We, too, have suffered, and perhaps we are suffering now. Even if we believe no one could possibly know how we feel, consider this: God knows. And He also knows that happiness is just around the corner.

His Soothing Presence

*Even in my suffering I was comforted
because your promise gave me life.*

PSALM 119:50 GNT

The first question is why. Why did this happen? Even if we can pinpoint a likely cause, however, our suffering remains. So God answers our "why?" not with an explanation, but with His soothing presence, His compassion and understanding, and His assurance that He is still in control. Our faith matters, and God invites us to put our trust in Him. Our feelings matter, too, and God yearns to bring us His comfort and peace.

SURRENDER

Wide Open

You may make your plans,
but God directs your actions.

PROVERBS 16:9 GNT

The opportunity is gone. It's as if someone has slammed a door and it's closed
tight. We can't help but stand and stare,
trying to understand what happened. And
our compassionate God stands right beside
us. When we're ready to let Him, He will
turn the eyes of our spirit to another door,
this one open to us—wide open. The moment we surrender our will to the will of
our loving God, we can discover all that's
waiting there for us.

Room for Serenity

Be still, and know that I am God.

PSALM 46:10 KJV

God yearns to fill us with His peace, but He often finds us reluctant to give up those things that hinder it. Things like gossip and status-seeking, competition and self-centeredness, busyness and insistence on our own way. If we let God's Spirit sweep these things away from our hearts and minds, there's room for serenity to move in. If we surrender ourselves to God's overwhelming love, our spirits are ready to receive His all-consuming and everlasting peace.

TEMPTATION

Opportunity

My brothers and sisters,
when you have many kinds of
troubles, you should be full of joy.

JAMES 1:2 NCV

God works for our good and turns even sinful desires to our benefit. When temptation comes our way, it's yet another opportunity for us to choose His commandments over our urges, and another chance to put in action our love for Him. Our Spirit-strengthened resistance shields us from spiritual danger and enables us to gain self-control and self-assurance. Temptation may trouble us, but deep peace is ours when we let Him turn our temptation to our gain.

He Leads

*We are instructed to turn from godless living
and sinful pleasures. We should
live in this evil world with wisdom,
righteousness, and devotion to God.*

TITUS 2:12 NLT

The longer we meditate on God's will and
purpose for our lives, the more aware we
become of things that pull us away from
Him. In the light of God's desires for us,
behaviors we never saw as harmful before,
now show up as hindrances to spiritual
growth. Giving in to "harmless" temptations no longer satisfies us, and there are
changes we want to make. This is God's
Spirit in us, speaking, and with His words,
He leads.

TIREDNESS

Wonders

*[God] gives strength to the weary
and increases the power of the weak.*

ISAIAH 40:29

Who among us doesn't know what it's
like to be tired—really tired? When fatigue
becomes a constant companion, it's time to
find a reliable source of refreshment and
relaxation. God's Spirit can do wonders
when given even five or ten minutes a day
to remind us of God's power in our lives
and His willingness to help us with our
needs and priorities. Tiredness slips away
when we place our burdens on Him and
lean on His ever-present strength.

Spiritual Refreshment

It is useless for you to work so hard from
early morning until late at night. . .
for God gives rest to his loved ones.

PSALM 127:2 NLT

Tiredness tells us it's time to get some rest. Yes, each of us has a limit, both physically and emotionally. Our gracious God, creator of body and spirit, uses tiredness for our good. It's His way of drawing us to Him so He can refresh us spiritually and His way of turning us to others for relaxation, spontaneity, laughter, and friendship. We may not like to feel tired, but sometimes it's the only way God can reach us when we're on the go!

TRADITIONS

Family of God

*Let us not neglect our meeting
together, as some people do,
but encourage one another.*

HEBREWS 10:25 NLT

Year after year we celebrate treasured
traditions with family and friends. As
members of God's family of believers, we
are blessed with many opportunities to celebrate together. Shared worship surrounds
us with the encouragement and love of
other believers, and holidays like Christ-
mas and Easter offer a special chance to
lift our hearts and voices together in songs
of praise. When we celebrate our spiritual
traditions, we share together the joy of be-
longing to the family of God.

Worthy Traditions

*The LORD is good and his love
endures forever; his faithfulness
continues through all generations.*

PSALM 100:5

All too often, the holidays we celebrate
turn into times of tension and stress. It's
through Spirit-inspired decision and
action that we can reshape our holiday
traditions. We can focus on what's
meaningful to us and the people we love,
and we can decline to participate in those
things that drain our time and energy.
Through our efforts, we can establish
traditions that bless us—traditions worthy
to be passed down to the next generation.

TRIALS

Inward Strength

*I consider that our present sufferings
are not worth comparing with the glory
that will be revealed in us.*

ROMANS 8:18

We're powerless to change the situation, or the consequences of doing so are unacceptable. This kind of trial forces us inward, where we're likely to find more strength than we ever knew we possessed. Daily time with God to focus on the issue renews our commitment to a God-pleasing response in the things we think, say, and do. Our patience amid such trials builds resilience, and our serenity in trying times works for peace wherever peace may find a willing heart.

Richly Blessed

[The Lord] said to me, "My grace is sufficient
for you, for My strength is
made perfect in weakness."

2 CORINTHIANS 12:9 NKJV

There are disturbing thoughts, unfortu-
nate personality traits, or seemingly un-
breakable habits or addictions. Even in trials of heart, mind, and emotions, our Great
Physician is there. He opens His arms to
us and invites us to rest in His peace. We
discover that despite our personal burdens, God calls us His beloved daughters.
His Spirit works within us and blesses us
richly. We find our strength in Him alone
as we walk on with Him to victory.

TRUST

Companionship

Those who know your name put
their trust in you, for you, O Lord,
have not forsaken those who seek you.

PSALM 9:10 NRSV

Very often we find it difficult to trust: We have been hurt too many times. Yet lack of trust keeps us from the close, comfortable relationships we long for. God's Spirit draws us toward others because He desires companionship for us as we walk our life's path. He wants only peace for us as He brings the right people alongside us, who can help and support, encourage, and love us as we learn to trust again.

Securely in Him

I trust in your love. My heart is happy
because you saved me. I sing to the Lord
because he has taken care of me.

PSALM 13:5–6 NCV

When we trust someone it shows in our
actions. We can depend on and confide in
that person without worry of betrayal. Our
trust in God expresses itself in action, too.
Trust compels us to rely on His promises
and take Him at His word when He says
He'll bless us, strengthen us, and comfort
us. Trust in God enables us to live at peace
with Him, with ourselves, and with others,
because our faith rests securely in Him.

VIOLENCE

Free Hearts

*[God] has rescued us from the power
of darkness and transferred us into the kingdom
of his beloved Son, in whom we have
redemption, the forgiveness of sins.*

COLOSSIANS 1:13–14 NRSV

Peace and violence do not go together,
and God is a God of peace. To the tears of
violence, He brings His words of comfort
and compassion, and to the wounds of violence, He brings the balm of emotional and
spiritual healing. To the scars of violence,
He enables forgiveness. Through forgiveness, violence loses its power to inflict
more harm. Forgiveness frees our hearts
and minds to live again as women worthy of
honor, dignity, and love.

Peaceful Hearts

The fruit of that righteousness
will be peace; its effect will be
quietness and confidence forever.

ISAIAH 32:17

Peace begins from within, and where there's anger, violence, hatred, and fighting, there is no peace. That's why God's Spirit works in our hearts to root out those things that make our inner peace impossible. Then, with His genuine peace firmly established within us, we cannot help but express His sublime gift in our homes, communities, and workplaces. A world where each heart possesses His peace is the surest road to a world at peace.

WORK

Genuine Joy and Fulfillment

*Surely the Lord your God has blessed
you in all your undertakings.*

DEUTERONOMY 2:7 NRSV

All honest work pleases God. Unlike the world around us, God does not judge on status or pay scale, or on whether our work takes us around the world or no farther than our kitchen sink. Instead, God looks at our hearts, where He delights to find integrity, patience, honesty, and trustworthiness. He knows that from this heart genuine joy flows, and wherever joy is present, there is fulfillment in work and peace in spirit.

God's Definition of Work

We are what he has made us, created in Christ Jesus for good works, which God prepared beforehand to be our way of life.

EPHESIANS 2:10 NRSV

Deadlines and long to-do lists, endless chores and household demands all give work a bad name! Yet God intends our work to not only provide for our needs and the needs of others, but to bring us a sense of fulfillment and satisfaction. When we go to Him and "unload" at the end of the day, God makes it His work to help and support us and enable us to make His definition of work a reality in our lives.

SCRIPTURE INDEX

Exodus

34:14 117

Leviticus

19:11 52

Deuteronomy

2:7 206

4:7 151

20:3–4 188

31:6 70

31:8 63

Joshua

1:5 148

1:9 62

24:15 159

1 Samuel

12:22 164

2 Chronicles

20:17 85

Esther

4:14 121

Psalms

3:3 42

9:10 202

13:5–6 203

20:4 95

23:4 24

25:1–2 173

25:8–9 108

30:11 25

32:2 104

34:17 74

34:18 30

34:19 13

37:7 55

37:25 15

46:10 193

51:6 140

51:10 189

73:23 122

73:28 131

85:8, 10 5

100:5 199

103:12 134

111:1 100

112:1 22

119:28 68

119:50 191

119:73 139

119:105 177

119:130 145

127:2 197

130:1–2 130

138:7 10

138:8 120

139:14 179

143:8 64

Proverbs

1:7 96

3:3 80

3:5–6 112

3:9–10 129

11:2 155

11:25 93

14:1 82

14:30 110

15:28 132

15:31–32 46

16:9 192

16:24 184

17:9 89

17:27 38

22:6 34

31:30 21

Ecclesiastes

4:6 116

7:9 160

Isaiah

12:2 152

26:3 146

30:15 170

30:18 31

30:21 113

32:17 205

40:29 196

41:10 84

41:13 57

44:22 103

46:4 14

49:23 58

55:7 162

Jeremiah

6:16 99

29:11 90

33:2, 6 12

33:8 163

Lamentations

3:22 79

3:25 106

Ezekiel

2:6 72

16:63 87

Hosea

6:3 97

Micah

6:8 49

Nahum

1:7 78

Malachi

4:2 153

Matthew

5:4 59

6:20 137

6:33 158

11:28 11

12:35 185

19:14 35

20:26 118

25:40 174

28:20 69

Luke

6:36 111

6:37 28

12:15 128

16:10 105

16:13 136

John

3:36 76

8:31–32 60

10:29 39

12:26 180

14:1 56

14:27 6

15:15 88

16:33 .... 43, 144

Acts

1:4 54

Romans

3:3–4.................................... 67

3:23–24................................. 135

6:23 77

8:18 200

8:28 51

8:38–39................................. 61

12:3 154

12:5 123

12:17–18 44

13:1 23

14:12 9

15:4 176

1 Corinthians

6:18 138

7:32 19

7:34 182

9:26 36

10:13 187

12:5 181

13:4 115

13:5 161

15:3 16

15:57 186

16:14 126

2 Corinthians

1:4 124

1:5 71

4:18 107

5:9 94

7:10 165

8:21 169

9:7 92

12:9 . . . . , ... 201

Galatians

2:6 20

5:22–23 157

5:25 32

Ephesians

1:4 29

2:4–5 178

2:8–9 37

2:10 207

4:15 47

4:24 53

4:26–27 17

4:31 27

5:3 183

6:10 83

Philippians

1:10 102

4:11 41

Colossians

1:13–14 204

2:6–7 48

3:8 65

3:9–10 125

3:13 86

3:23 141

4:2 150

1 Thessalonians

1:3 156

5:18 101

2 Thessalonians

3:3 81

1 Timothy

4:12 119

6:6 40

Titus

2:12 195

Hebrews

6:1 171

10:14 147

10:25 198

12:15 26

13:4 127

13:8 33

James

1:2 194

1:4 149

1:5 172

1:6 66

1:25 143

3:18 166

4:8 75

4:10 109

4:15 91

1 Peter

1:22 114

2:11 50

2:12 168

3:15 ...., ... 45

4:13 ,.................................. 190

5:7 18

5:8-9.................................. 73

2 Peter

3:18 133

1 John

1:9 8

2:2 175

2:17 98

5:3 142

Revelation

3:20 167